The Cleveland Press

Fair today; fair and warmer tomorrow

ISSUE NO. 17229   CLEVELAND, MONDAY, AUGUST 8, 1932   Entered as second-class matter, Post Office, Cleveland, O.

GOODRICH SPECIAL

PRICE THREE CENTS

GOODRICH FAMILY ROMPS AT BEACH

EUCLID BEACH PARK – A SECOND LOOK

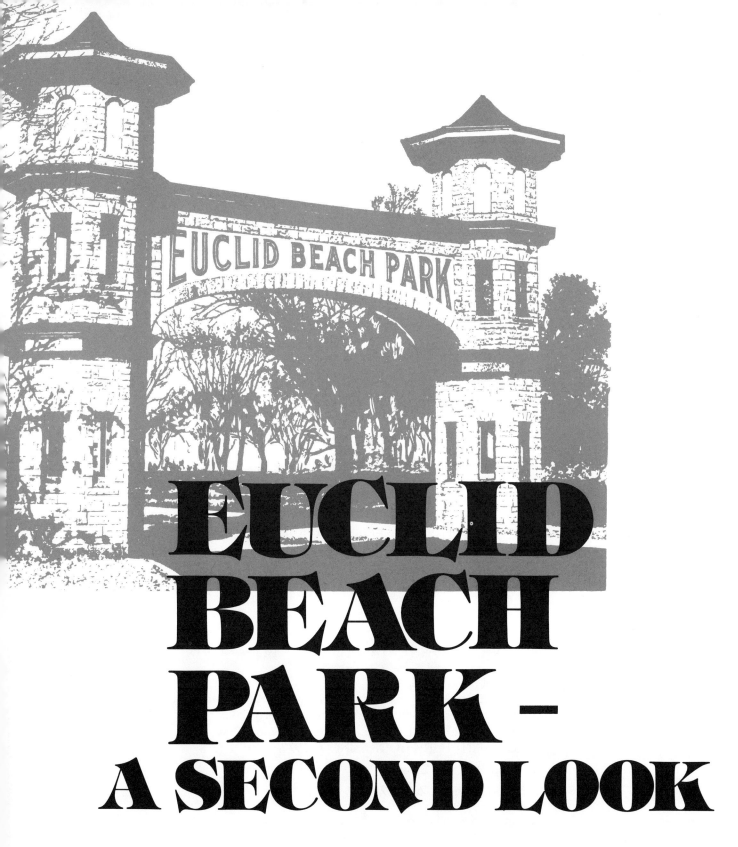

EUCLID BEACH PARK – A SECOND LOOK

by

AMUSEMENT PARK BOOKS, INC.
which is . . .
Lee O. Bush
Edward C. Chukayne
Russell Allon Hehr
Richard F. Hershey

AP
BOOKS, INC.
Mentor, Ohio 44060

PRINTED IN THE UNITED STATES OF AMERICA

ISBN 0-935408-01-0
LIBRARY OF CONGRESS
CATALOG CARD NO.: 79-55562
Euclid Beach Park.

OHIO: Amusement Park Books

234 p.

7910   790924

PUBLISHED BY AMUSEMENT PARK BOOKS, INC.
Mentor, Ohio 44060

LIBRARY OF CONGRESS CATALOGING IN PUBLICATION DATA

Amusement Park Books.
   EUCLID BEACH PARK—A SECOND LOOK / by Amusement
Park Books, Inc., which is Lee O. Bush, Edward C. Chukayne,
Russell Allon Hehr, Richard F. Hershey—Mentor, Ohio;
AMUSEMENT PARK BOOKS, INC. © 1979.

   viii, p. 234; ill. ; 29 cm.

   Bibliography; p. 201-202
   Includes index.
   ISBN 0-935408-01-0

      1. Euclid Beach Park, Ohio—History   1. Title.
   GV1853.E9A48   1979   790'.068'0977132   79-55562

DEDICATION

A multitude of people created, shaped, maintained and sustained Euclid Beach Park. Some dedicated their entire working lives to it. Some were young; some were middle-aged; some were old. Some did menial tasks; some did spectacular tasks. Some worked there for an hour; some worked there for months; some worked there for years or even a lifetime.

To those people whose work and devotion became transformed into the Park's image, we dedicate our second volume on Euclid Beach Park.

It is for them we took a SECOND LOOK.

> Lee O. Bush
> Edward C. Chukayne
> Russell Allon Hehr
> Richard F. Hershey

(Courtesy of MOSER/O'NEIL, INC.—ARROW DEVELOPMENT CO.)

INTRODUCTION

In the early part of this century nearly every American city had its amusement park. To enter such parks as Cleveland's Euclid Beach was to be transported into an illusionary world of fantasy and thrilling rides. The older entertainments of theatre and circus, for example, allowed for the nineteenth century American to witness a magical event yet stay within his ordered, nineteenth century lifestyle. But the new amusement parks which developed at the turn of the century let the visitor partake of an experience best delineated by E. E. Cummings in the 1920s when he was describing Coney Island's world renowned attractions:

> Coney has a distinct drop on both theatre and circus. Whereas at the theatre we are merely deceived, at Coney we deceive ourselves. Whereas at the circus we are merely spectators of the impossible, at Coney we ourselves perform impossible feats. . . . THE AUDIENCE IS THE PERFORMANCE, and vice versa.

There were many basic changes occurring in the American way of life that set the stage for the emergence of the amusement park and which, historically, made it a cultural symbol of the new American lifestyle. Life in nineteenth century America was in many ways more "Victorian" than the England ruled by Queen Victoria. Genteel culture arbitrated public taste but by the end of the century impatience with the old restraints surfaced among a new generation of Americans — the urban working class. Leisure, once spent in edifying activities of moral and social value, was now the new market for entrepreneurs who found a swelling urban population with increased time and spending power.

The most striking expression of this change was in the new amusement parks which were developing just when the twentieth century arrived. Earlier public parks had sought to provide a contemplative rural retreat but the new commercial parks were called amusement parks because they aimed to amuse rather than to uplift. Here were the mechanical amusements in an industrial age with which the visitor could associate. Here, too, were grandiose and exotic settings from which he could escape his drab world. No longer was he the spectator but rather an intimate participant in the spectacle about him. Now the pleasure seeker was the actor upon the stage.

As a harbinger of a new mass culture, the amusement park was not just a symbol of fun and frolic but also of major changes in America's manners and morals. Yet even the amusement park was eclipsed within a few decades by newer symbols such as the automobile (replacing the trolley which had taken the public to the parks; now they drove to roadhouses and drive-ins) and, closer to our own time, television. The amusement park did not die out, of course, but its importance and meaning changed in the minds of Americans. Disneyland's opening in 1955 caused a renaissance in the park business and the last decade has seen several huge theme parks open. Coupled with this has been increasing public sentiment for the old wooden merry-go-round and a mania for roller coasters.

Scholarly attention is now being given to the history of popular entertainments because they can help us understand who we are and what our past was like. The amusement parks which developed at the turn of the century can tell us much about the change from a genteel, rural culture to an urban, industrial age. Americans did not seek to escape the raucousness of the new age for they went to the amusement park where they found a familiar setting of crowds, mechanical wonders, and rapidly changing experiences. If they escaped to anything, it was to an exotic world but not a foreign one. They had fled the poor rural life for the promise of the city and though they might not yet have realized their dream, they could find it for a day at amusement parks like Euclid Beach.

Because of the great significance of the early amusement parks in American life, we should not forget about them. Books such as this one preserve the history and memories of some of our parks but precious few of the surviving parks retain even a hint of their past. The day may not be far off when an old park is restored as a living historic museum. Clevelanders have lost Euclid Beach but it lives vigorously in the memories of many. The only tangible reminder is the old entranceway and history-conscious Clevelanders have done well to preserve the landmark as a symbol with an historical site marker. It reminds us all not only of a change in the American way of life but of good amusement enjoyed by generations of Clevelanders.

Richard W. Flint

PREFACE

During the many years we worked on EUCLID BEACH PARK IS CLOSED FOR THE SEASON our constant aim was to bring together all the pieces we could gather about the Great Old Park in an inclusive, thoroughly researched, documentary book complete with bibliography, appendices, index, etc. — "a pattern for future books on amusement parks."

Our book, once it was published, begat a sforzando of responses from collectors, former park employees and interested laymen. Our telephones began ringing. Individuals would ask us questions like: "Did you know that . . .?"; "Perhaps you forgot to mention . . .?"; "Would you like to include . . .?"; "Is there more on . . .?" In essence the questions indicated there was more material. "Would we? / We must!" do a second volume.

A second volume? We were well aware that some of the secondary material had been deleted from EUCLID BEACH PARK IS CLOSED FOR THE SEASON at the last minute to keep the cost within limits. A second volume? A second look?

We made surveys to which the people replied: "Yes, there *is* a definite interest." "Yes, let us give you some *added* material!"

A second volume! Slowly we realized that though the bulldozers had rent assunder the Grand Old Park called Euclid Beach; even though the land had been violated with other than amusement park debris; even though commercialism had chewed at its doorstep; even though cool green trees had mercilessly been cut down to make way for hot red signs and dusty parking lots — in spite of all, in the memories of many, many, *many,* people, the 75 and 93/100 acres which was Euclid Beach still lived on. Yes, let us take a second look! we concluded.

What is more, the younger generation (we are talking here about youngsters barely tall enough in "age" to qualify for the height requirement necessary to get on the rides at amusement parks, as well as teen-agers) showed a great interest in the park. No one of them knew Euclid Beach other than through parents, grandparents or our book. The number of amusement park enthusiasts is growing rapidly among the younger generation. As testimony to this the American Coaster Enthusiasts organization has tripled in two years. The National Carrousel Association has continued to attract all ages.

Yes, there would be a second volume — a second look. Our aims, we decided, would be the same as stated in the preface of the first volume. The format would be the same. The colors of the cover and dust jacket would be the same. (This, in order that the two volumes could be shelved side by side.)

The emphasis in the second volume, it was finally decided, would be more on the pictorial side augmented by captions, newspaper ads, articles, and selected printed memorabilia. However, we wanted our second volume to be complete within itself for those who might have access to it alone. Its emphasis, however, would be more on visual reminiscing than by text.

All material in the second volume would be new! No material would be duplicated from volume one. New appendices would be added where new facts had been brought to light after the first book. Where material or pictures of an era, or location, or ride were sparse in volume one, we have tried our utmost to ferret out more information or visual material. And that is how we arrived at our title — A SECOND LOOK.

Our conversations with former employees and persons at mall shows, lectures and special meetings yielded a wealth of new facts.

The bibliography would be extended to include newer publications on amusement parks. While some would not directly pertain to Euclid Beach, they would be relevant in that they would expand the horizon for future generations, and much of the material would apply indirectly.

We felt that the second volume should contain the master index for both, even though the first volume index is complete in itself. The master index will guide the reader to text and pictures in the first volume *and* the second by the use of parallel columns.

Once again we could not have dared a second volume had it not been for an overwhelming number of people and institutions who proferred their time and information.

Once again, as when we were putting together our first volume on Euclid Beach Park, we wish to acknowledge our gratitude to Doris Humphrey Mackley and Dudley Sherman Humphrey, III, the direct descendants of the family that "owned, operated, and rigidly maintained their high standards for the park from 1901 until its closing in 1969". Since 1977, when our first volume was published, they have accorded us much time and enthusiasm, verified many newfound facts, and once again allowed us access to their huge scrapbook on the park for an in-depth "second look".

What is more, we share with all the amusement park enthusiasts in praising these owners of great old Euclid Beach for continuing their heritage by establishing a new amusement park called Shady Lake in Streetsboro, Ohio. Many of the former rides have been lovingly refurbished and transplanted to the new park; indeed, many of the former operators of those rides at Euclid Beach are back on the job at Shady Lake. And STILL the family tradition goes on by instance on high standards, rigid maintenance and "nothing to depress or demoralize". Each year the new park expands with a blending of old and new. Thus the essence of Euclid Beach lives on transported to another shore; a kudos is in order.

Harry Luikart, photographer as well as collector of Euclid Beach memorabilia deserves a bravo for his expertise; his willingness to enlarge, make smaller, reprint, on a day and night basis has earned our undying thanks. He has let us use his studio for everything from photographing parts of the huge Humphrey scrapbook to holding meetings of the authors there. What is more his collection of things about the park has augmented the pleasures of this book. The spirit of Euclid Beach lives on in such a person!

Marjorie H. Kekic with her huge collection of primary source photos of the park has again delighted the authors and posterity by allowing the use of still more of them in this second volume. Her patience with us and all the problems involved in getting photos translated onto the pages of a book certainly show forth the graciousness of this understanding person.

Jan Cooch of Braum-Brumfield printers in Ann Arbor, Michigan has listened, advised and tolerated our tons of questions and over-anxious temperments in order to bring together all the material to be translated into print; she it is who transformed the disparate into a cohesive book — not once, but twice. Laurels to this astute and efficient woman.

Dr. Robert Cartmel, foremost authority and writer on roller coasters has continued to share his vast storehouse of facts and pictures with us. He has lent us his enthusiastic support while we "birthed" these two books.

Many former employees (some of them still working for the Humphreys at their new Shady Lake Park) deserve our thanks:

Art Steele, operator of the THRILLER, whose chant "Wait 'till the train stops" ended our first volume,"reopened" the park for us with his memories, his pictures and his fervent love of the hallowed acres.

Mr. Walter Williams was willing, once again, to dig into his "bag of remember-ances" about the park. He and his wife have lived at the park for most of their lives.

Bob Lupton and Marty Opalk were anxious to share their observations of the "old days".

Thomas Barensfeld, Librarian of the Cleveland Press Library and author has given us enthus-iastic support. His timely articles on "old" Cleveland and its architecture as well as his articles on Cleveland Amusement Parks has helped our cause and indirectly that of amusement park buffs all over the country.

Lawrence V. Lindberg, our attorney, has endured listening to, advising about and resolving all the legal problems and entanglements authors and publishers get into and out of.

Gerald M. Appel has expertly guided us through the maze of financial and tax problems in order that we might "get on" with the business of writing and publishing.

Robert Liederbach has been a real friend to all of us by his pleasant ways and helpful advice on many publishing matters. He has been a great help with both volumes.

Tom Polk, Program Director at WEWS-TV, shares our enthusiasm for amusement parks. He sacrifices much time in investigating them. He has helped spread the interest in Euclid Beach by his TV special, thus encouraging many people to contact us and consequently reveal unknown facets of the park.

Ted Alexander has aided our cause many times through radio programs on station WBBG, which in turn, have reached people with new material for our second book. His wife Barbara has championed our cause by aiding at several shows, contacting people and charming them to "volunteer".

Mr. and Mrs. Robert Levine, owners of Publix Book Mart, often counselled us and offered many suggestions on the book business and publishing.

Richard Wickens of the National Carousel Association has been most helpful on matters deal-ing with carousels. He graciously photographed, in great detail, the old Euclid Beach Carrousel at Old Orchard Beach, Maine.

Richard Munch, Clarence Hintze and Allen Ambrosini of the American Coaster Enthusiasts have been of great help.

Ron Antonick and his family helped in delivery and promotional efforts at a moment's notice. Through their labors at moving "Laughing Sal" hither and yon, many older person's memories were touched and the younger generation became acquainted with this tangible relic of Euclid Beach Park.

William Stoneback, descendant of Howard Stoneback, famous engineer and creator of rides at the park, has furnished us pictures and information.

Jeff Mach and Douglas Kotris with their expertise in films and photography have been of much assistance.

James ("Jack") E. Robinson has patiently aided by keeping archival materials in proper files and from going astray, by "hearing" constant revisions and trial runs, and enduring assorted tribulations.

David Humphrey Scott, with his never ending enthusiasm for things Euclid Beach, has con-tinued to dig for information and contacts. His enthusiasm is infectious; his crusade for the park's memory is dauntless!

Mr. and Mrs. Charles Sweide, Jr. and Gary Sweide were most helpful in talking with people to "dig" for information and to promote interest in our books.

Martha Cedar volunteered valuable archival material.

Ann Tompkins has typed and retyped the manuscript, suffering from almost illegible hand writing problems and hasty temperaments. She certainly deserves a "second ride" on the THRILLER.

The School of Fine Arts, Willoughby, Ohio deserves our thanks.

The audio-visual aspect of Euclid Beach has been greatly augmented; many films, slides, records and tapes of the park came to light after our first volume was published. The following people helped in this effort.

David (Dave) Humphrey Scott allowed us to view his collection of original films of the park taken by his father again and again and *again*. We thank him.

William L. Schurk, Audio Librarian; Head of Popular Culture Library at Bowling Green State University, Ohio, came forth with some original records used with "Laughing Sal" and "Sam" and transferred them onto tape.

A. Wayne Boggs searched, rescued and assembled on tape old sounds of the park which had been waiting to be heard on old records, tapes, etc.

Chuck J. Russell of Massillon, Ohio spent many hours travelling to Cleveland in order that he could bring his movies and gleanings of old Euclid Beach sounds to ears young and old. Often he and A. Wayne Boggs combined their forces to produce "you are there" type audio-visual material, and a film used at mall shows.

Norm Worgull had preserved many artifacts and memorabilia from the beach. He and his son Jim Worgull, who had collected excellent pictorial material, shared them with the authors.

Fred Griffith of Channel 5 TV on both his "Morning" and "Afternoon Exchange" shows aided greatly in spreading the news about the park and the book — causing many people to come forth with new information.

The following media people deserve our special thanks:

Tom Ott — Journal Newspapers
Bruce Hackett — Sun Newspapers
Norman N. Mlachak — Cleveland Press
Ed Fisher — WBBG
Tony Petkovsek — WZAK
Linn Sheldon — Channel 43
Leo D'Arcy — WELV
Fred Griffith — Channel 5
Tom Polk — Channel 5
June Williams — Call and Post
Joan Gestl — News-Herald
Painesville Telegraph
The Last Word — Chagrin Falls, Ohio

Our patient wives have once again endured innumerable encroachments into their family and personal existences and yet emerged with invaluable smiles. Stephanie Bush, Carolyn Chukayne, Linda Hershey, we salute you and thank you.

Catherine Lehman and Laura Chukayne, daughters of Ed Chukayne, and his son Charles ("Chuck") Lehman supported promotional efforts and found additional materials for this volume. Chuck spent many hours setting up sound systems for numerous displays promoting the first book. As an engineer for WBBG he provided an expertly spliced tape of "Laughing Sal's" voice made from original records for use whenever she was on public display.

September, Nancy and Steve Bush, daughters and son of Lee Bush, have been of assistance at many public functions that have represented Euclid Beach and the book, also, their patience and encouragement is invaluable.

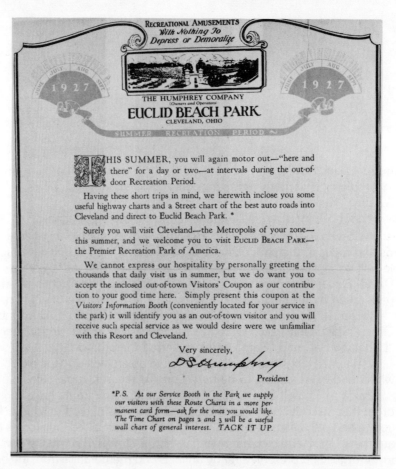

RECREATIONAL AMUSEMENTS
With Nothing To
Depress or Demoralize

1927   1927

THE HUMPHREY COMPANY
(Owners and Operators)
EUCLID BEACH PARK
CLEVELAND, OHIO

SUMMER RECREATION PERIOD

THIS SUMMER, you will again motor out—"here and there" for a day or two—at intervals during the out-of-door Recreation Period.

Having these short trips in mind, we herewith inclose you some useful highway charts and a Street chart of the best auto roads into Cleveland and direct to Euclid Beach Park. *

Surely you will visit Cleveland—the Metropolis of your zone—this summer, and we welcome you to visit EUCLID BEACH PARK—the Premier Recreation Park of America.

We cannot express our hospitality by personally greeting the thousands that daily visit us in summer, but we do want you to accept the inclosed out-of-town Visitors' Coupon as our contribution to your good time here. Simply present this coupon at the *Visitors' Information Booth* (conveniently located for your service in the park) it will identify you as an out-of-town visitor and you will receive such special service as we would desire were we unfamiliar with this Resort and Cleveland.

Very sincerely,

President

P.S.   At our Service Booth in the Park we supply our visitors with these Route Charts in a more permanent card form—ask for the ones you would like. The Time Chart on pages 2 and 3 will be a useful wall chart of general interest.   TACK IT UP.

We also wish to show the greatest appreciation to the following gracious contributors and supporters:

Sister Ancilla of Parmadale, John Boris, Jerry Bowman, Robert Calaghan, The families of Frank and Robert Chukayne, Robert Cigoy, Beth Cooper, Honey Cramer, Denise Eiermann, Rod Ehrhart, Ruth Florence, Eunice Foote, Michael Fuerst, M. Gandee, George Gecik, Neva Hansen, Jean and Linda Hochevar, Franklin Kotnik, Chuck Lawson, Robert J. Leist, Mary Ann Maggio, John Marino, Harry "Pepper" Martin, Edna (Ott) Maurer, Gregory Mihelh, Judge Robert F. Niccum, James L. Nickerson, Al Phillips, Harlan Radford, Jim Rajcan, Don Ressler, James Ruple, Tom Satyrshur, Paul & Agnes Schwesinger, Laura Swackhamer, Patty Souvain, Randall Tiedman, Bill Vidmar, Richard C. Walter, Don Woods, Willis Zeitz.

And once again the authors would address the Park:

"There are so many relics nobody ever finds them all," says the old poem. Euclid Beach Park we have gathered up still more pieces of you. We have taken them and assembled them in a new second volume about you. We never could have found them all, but we did find enough to keep your memory alive in our two volumes.

We loved you. Young, old, in-between, all loved you. Those on shores beyond human reach loved you. You gave to us the excitement-filled, pleasurable pauses we needed on our way from here to eternity. To those who knew you not, your story will live on in these pages; for us who knew you, we offer you our second look.

Cleveland, Ohio, September, 1979
AMUSEMENT PARK BOOKS, Inc.
Lee O. Bush
Edward C. Chukayne
Russell Allon Hehr
Richard F. Hershey

CONTENTS

WAY BACK

(Bill Vidmar)

WHEN

'Way Back When . . .

"Grampa" could not even remember . . .
people dressed up to be in public . . .
cars and aeroplanes were new things . . .
America had a dream in its eye . . .
Euclid Beach Park became a local and national institution
that made part of that dream come true . . .

(Illus. 1) This extraordinary 180° picture of the Euclid Beach DANCE PAVILION shows one of the crowds during the early heyday (c. 1912). The second floor balcony and outside stairway were later changed.

(Illus. 2) The original downtown "Hole-in-the-Wall" popcorn stand in May's Drug Store on Public Square, Cleveland, Ohio (circa 1894). This was the site of the original Humphrey Company success and subsequent trip to Euclid Beach Park.

(The Humphrey Company)

(Illus. 3) The growing business now also sold "pure cream candy". The taste of the CANDY KISS was to become a legend. The second floor shows the taffy pulling as originally done by hand.

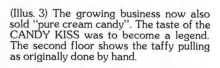

(The Humphrey Company)

A LITTLE HISTORY

EUCLID BEACH PARK is owned and operated by The Humphrey Co., the largest manufacturers and retailers of pop corn and pull candy in the world, and they are the originators and inventors of all implements, methods and arrangements used in this business.

About a dozen years ago this family (ladies and children, too), without a dollar in capital and badly in debt, started popping and retailing pop corn from push carts on the streets, and at this date we feel that we can claim with modesty that no other concern in Cleveland is better or more favorably known.

Pure material and great care in making our products, as well as everlasting vigilance in working out the resort problem is cause of success.

We are especially fitted to take care of the biggest picnics, reunions, societies, clubs, etc. We can accommodate more people under roof than any other resort in the land.

Euclid Beach has more real amusement features and all are safer, better cared for and all devices better made than can be found anywhere else.

Some of them are :
Dancing
Bathing
Boating
Bowling
Base Ball
Box Ball
Scenic Railroad
Aerial Swing
Roller Skating
Moving Pictures
Figure Eight
Carousel
Merrygorounds
Ocean Wave
Pony Track
Then we have
Camping
Pop Corn
Photo Studio
Picnic Grounds
2,000 Feet of
  Sand Beach
Fine Groves

THIS IS WHAT DID IT

OUR CORN-POPPER

UNDER FIRST MANAGEMENT WE TOOK IN $2,500 FOR POP CORN AND PULL CANDY AT EUCLID BEACH. FIRST YEAR, UNDER OUR OWN MANAGEMENT, POP CORN AND PULL CANDY TOOK IN $10,000. MUCH MORE NOW.

OUR EMPLOYEES ARE OF THE BEST CLASS AND USUALLY WELL FITTED FOR THEIR TASKS. MANY POSITIONS ARE OCCUPIED BY STUDENTS WHO ARE WORKING THEIR WAY THROUGH THE SCHOOLS AND COLLEGES

A LITTLE TALK

EUCLID BEACH PARK under its first management (five years) attracted very limited attendance and resulted in complete failure financially.

The natural advantages and some of the features were good, but they had beer, freaks, fakes, chance games, questionable shows, palmists, etc., (made a bid for everybody and got nobody). During that time we had the pop corn concession in the park and saw where they, like nearly all resort people, were mistaken.

We had faith in the people. We knew, and wanted to prove that if given an equal opportunity, almost every one would "class up" on the good side, and results show it.

Fortunately, when they failed we were able to take the park, and under our management it has earned the reputation of being the most moral, temperate, orderly, safe, and beautiful, also the best patronized and best paying and largest family summer resort in America.

Visitors here experience at once a clean, pure atmosphere of security, comfort, good will, and freedom from congestion or anything demoralizing or depressing; no tendency toward the morbid, immoral or intemperate.

Our utmost and constant endeavor is to have everything of an uplifting and elevating character.

BIRD'S-EYE VIEW OF CAMP GROUNDS

EUCLID BEACH CONTAINS 80 ACRES.   THOUSANDS OF PEOPLE CAMP IN MOST COMPLETE HOUSE TENTS.   GAS, WATER, AND BEST SANITARY EFFECTS

(The Humphrey Company)

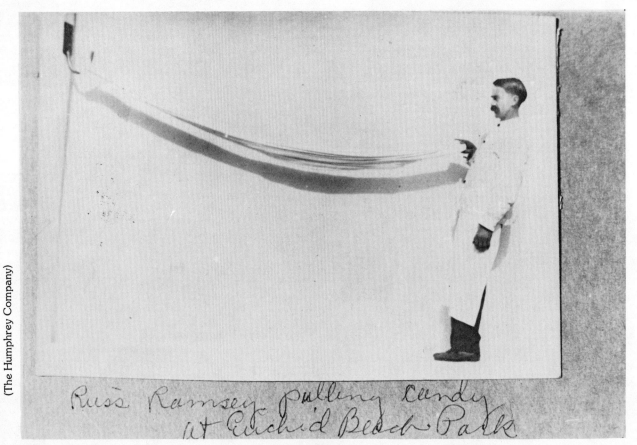

(Illus. 5) Russ Ramsey was a deadly shot with a length of taffy—he hardly ever missed. His job was taken over by machines which offered no less a fascinating scene during later days at Euclid Beach.

(Illus. 6) The horse and pony were still basic to American life in the early part of the century. They were basic as part of the park also.

(Illus. 7) The Circle Swing was installed with wicker gondola Biplane type cars replaced the gondolas and the ride was re named AEROPLANES in 1927. Finally, it became the ROCKE SHIPS when stainless steel "Buck Rodgers" type conveyance were put on the ride in 1938. Originally riders boarded direct from the ground.

(Illus. 7)

6

(Illus. 8) Ready to ride, these men do not seem terrified of the gentle dips of the FIGURE EIGHT. Details of the popular Philadelphia Toboggan ride cars and side friction board are evident here.

(The Humphrey Company)

(Illus. 9) The WORLD THEATRE (early in the century) was a place to witness wondrous new marvels such as motion pictures.

(Illus. 10) Although the Euclid Beach Hotel was not on the property of the park, many visitors and employees patronized it. The hotel was located across East 156th Street (west) overlooking Lake Erie.

(Russell Allon Hehr Collection)

AFTER a long, tedious drive, when you're dust laden and tired, what a relief it is to find a clean, home-like hotel, where the transient guest's comfort is the first consideration.

That's why you will want to stop in Cleveland at the Euclid Beach Hotel, attractively located next to Euclid Beach Park, on the shore of beautiful Lake Erie, eight miles east of Cleveland's Public Square.

The restfulness of this ideal spot, away from the noise and bustle of a large city, will strongly appeal to every member of your party.

A dining room now connects Euclid Beach Hotel. The menu provides varied sumptuous meals — special steak and fish dinners — home cooking to please your appetite.

All conveniences for club entertainments, card parties, out of town guests and tourists accommodation. Ample parking facilities for any occasion.

Reservations requested by phone or correspondence.

[Rates $1.50 per single and up.]

MRS. WALKER
EUCLID BEACH HOTEL
BEULAH PARK, CLEVELAND, OHIO
KENMORE 0418

(Robert Cigoy Collection)

(Illus. 11) Ladies and gentlemen in dress of the day strolled near the DANCE PAVILION on the wooden promenade (later to be a concrete walkway utilizing the Humphrey concrete pouring technique). The CARROUSEL is in the background.

(Ruth Florence)

(Illus. 12) Yes, there really was a BEACH at the park on the shores of Lake Erie, a really wide and clean BEACH with REALLY clean water to swim in.

(Illus. 14) Currier was a name of long standing in musical circles and at the Park. This early ad shows some of the places Currier's Band and Orchestra had been featured.

(The Humphrey Company)

(Illus. 13) The Telling-Belle Vernon Picnic of 1913 featured a twins contest. Here some contestants are shown near the LOG CABIN. This building was often used as a picnic headquarters from its reconstruction at the Beach in 1901 until the Park's closing. (The LOG CABIN was originally the Forestry Building at the 1901 Pan-American Exposition at Buffalo, New York).

(Edna Maurer (Ott)

(Richard F. Hershey Collection)

(Illus. 15) The outdoor WHIP and the loading station building of the SCENIC RAILWAY were two familiar features of the Beach in the early years.

Souvenir Edition.

EUCLID BEACH NEWS. Cleveland
Sixth City

VOL. III. NO. 14.   EUCLID BEACH PARK, OHIO. FRIDAY, SEPTEMBER 1, 1911.   10 Cents Per Copy.

D. S. HUMPHREY
PRES.

D. H. HUMPHREY
GEN. MGR.

Giving the Humble Beginning of the Humphreys---The Story of a Fortune Built Upon a Popcorn Foundation.

A fortune built upon a popcorn foundation!

"Unstable," you say. Not necessarily.

Popcorn, in the case of the Humphrey Brothers, has made the best fig of building material. It has built an unsuccessful and obscure amusement park to a place unique in the history of the summer amusement business. It has opened attractive refreshment booths throughout the city, built substantial homes and finally erected a beautiful and costly skating emporium, offering lovers of the sport the largest artificial ice surface in the world.

And all of this since 1891, the date when the Humphrey family moved to Cleveland from the country after the mortgage on their farm had been foreclosed.

The mainstays of the family in those days were D. S. Humphrey, president of The Humphrey Company, and D. H. Humphrey, its general manager. These young men, impelled by the urgent need confronting their families, turned their hands to the first work that offered. They were unskilled and could command no employment other than that of day laborers. After many rebuffs they were

at last successful in obtaining jobs as teamsters, work which they followed for two years.

Then came the turning point in their careers. One of the brothers invented a new-fangled corn-popper. They tried to sell the patent outright, offering it in one instance as low as $25.00. Then they manufactured a few poppers and tried to sell them, but with no more success. Finally they got a little hot under the collar.

"If we can't find anyone who wants our poppers, we'll use 'em ourselves. We'll go into the popcorn business on our own hook," they declared with emphasis, embellished perhaps with a few gentle expletives.

And they did. Fitting out little band wagons, now familiar on Cleveland streets, the two Humphrey brothers popped their corn and trundled the carts from house to house and street corner to street corner, selling five cents' worth here and five cents' worth there. Customers grew plentiful after a while. They liked the Humphrey brand. The Humphrey popcorn was different. It was more crisp and better buttered. So the business grew and the nickels multiplied into dollars. The vending business continued for three years.

Fortified with a modest capital, the Humphreys then leased a part of May's drug store at the corner of Ontario street and the Square, a stand which they still hold. This proved a gold mine at the very start, and has since been a steady contributor to the exchequer of the company.

In 1901, after having taken several little flyers in the amusement game, with more or less success, the Humphreys bought Euclid Beach Park. Up until this time Euclid Beach had been operated with a ten-cent gate admission and a German village annex. The Humphreys tore down the fence, made the entrance free and threw out the beer. Their judgment in these particulars was immediately vindicated by the immediate influx of picnics and general patronage. Under the old regime Euclid Beach had been practically a failure. Under the Humphrey plan it became, within the space of a few years, one of the most conspicuously successful amusement resorts of the entire country. The Humphreys at the very outset upset many of the traditions of the summer amusement business and brought surprise, not to say consternation, to veteran park men everywhere.

They have been generous, almost

lavish, in the money spent for new features. The best amusement devices have been installed and one of the greatest dancing halls ever constructed has accommodated thousands upon thousands of merry dancers. In 1907 a new scenic railway, costing upwards of $25,000, the longest and best road of the kind ever built, was installed. Its patronage justified the outlay.

The latest incursion of this company in the amusement field has been the building of the beautiful Elysium ice skating rink at the corner of Fairmount and Euclid. The Elysium is the most spacious and elaborate rink ever constructed. It was thrown open to the public November 29, 1908, and its patronage has been enormous. When the Elysium was building, wiseacres shook their heads. "It will never pay," they said. But they were wrong again. The Elysium is paying and paying big. It seems to fill a long felt want. Society has endorsed it, the lovers of clean sports have endorsed it and that portion of the general public which enjoys healthful exercise combined with innocent fun has put the stamp of its approval upon it. Necessarily the Elysium is another Hum-

phrey success!

We would like to say more about Euclid Beach Park, but space will not permit us to. People from all parts of the world have visited it. Its reputation for being well managed and having clean amusements is known everywhere.

The business of the Humphrey Co. has increased each year and this present year's business is away ahead of any other year in the history of the company.

NONE LIKE EUCLID BEACH.

As a summer resort there is none in the world just like Euclid Beach Park. Five cents car fare is all it need cost anyone to go to Euclid Beach. If you bring your lunch with you the Humphrey Co. will furnish you table, seats, tablecloth, sugar, salt and dishes free. You can send your little children to the park, your wives and daughters unprotected, and no harm or insult will come to them. You will find here one of the best organized police forces in the country—not needed to quell disturbers, but to keep disturbances from occurring.

(The Humphrey Company)

EUCLID BEACH
IS NOW OPEN
HOW TO GET TO THE PARK

South of Scovill transfer from any intersecting line to East 105th St. cars, then retransfer to cars marked Euclid Beach at Luna Park.

North of Scovill transfer from any intersecting line to East 105th St. cars, take car marked Euclid Beach.

West Side Patrons transfer to any intersecting line at the Square north of and including Scovill, then retransfer to East 105th St. Take car marked Euclid Beach.

In all cases be sure to get suburban check· on East 105th Street (Euclid Beach cars).

(Illus. 18) It would seem that this ad could no longer aid anyone in getting to Euclid Beach Park.

(Illus. 17) To the "Beach"—in style! Gentlemen in straw hats, seated somewhat formally as they ride in the 1910 White Motor bus of 1½ tons. (White Motor Corp.)

ROARING THROUGH THE '20s...

(Illus. 19) This scene near the BUG also reveals the AEROPLANES in flight. The AVENUE THEATRE is to the left.

(Robert Callaghan Collection)

15

WAITING OUT THE '30s

(Robert Callaghan Collection)

(Illus. 20) "Clean recreation . . . Nothing to depress or demoralize." That's what the sign said on the face of the loading area for the trolley cars. This was a welcome thought for those who came to the park. Here a crowd waits for their street car at the Lakeshore Blvd. station. The time is the 20s.

ROARING THROUGH THE '20s, WAITING OUT THE '30s

America roared through the jazz age like a roller coaster rider holding onto his straw hat. It was a time that made the amusement parks classic.

When the ride and the roar suddenly came to an end, the country was let down by the Great Depression. The waiting was eased for many, just by the presence of Euclid Beach Park. Some saved their pennies to get to the Beach without a cent left to spend there.

What price wouldn't we give just to go and sit among the Sycamores with the gentle breezes off Lake Erie and hear the roar of the THRILLER!

(Illus. 21) They came by the thousands for a thrill. A "flivver" infested parking lot next to the THRILLER indicates a massive crowd. This area was usually used as a BALLFIELD. The year is 1924. The higher second hill of the THRILLER is visible.

(Kekic Collection)

(Kekic Collection)

(Illus. 22) In the '20s proper attire was always worn at the Beach. Conduct was proper or the violator was ejected from the park. (We've come a long way since then?) The parking lot appears to be full of "flivvers" as visitors enter the parking lot entrance near the LOG CABIN and the POST OFFICE. "Let's just sit down on a park bench and watch people."

(Illus. 22a) "Wow, look at that, free tickets to Euclid Beach"! What a great prize. We don't know how they won them but it's clear that it was special.

(Russell Allon Hehr Collection)

Corner of Dance Pavilion. More People Dance at Euclid Beach Than at Any Dance Hall in the World.

The Best Known Park in the World. At Right— Entrance to Park.

The 800-Foot Pier Where Thousands Seek Lake Breezes.

The Most Favorably Known Park in the World. Nothing Here to Depress or Demoralize

Center of Page—The Huge Ice Arena at the Elysium, 257 Feet Long and 100 Feet Wide.

We Beat Jack Frost. Perfect Ice at The Elysium at All Times.

The Humphrey Company
Purveyors of Amusement to the People of Cleveland

"To make Cleveland happy!" That in itself, is an ideal worth living up to, and it is the actual reason why the Humphrey Company is in existence. Winter and summer this Master Amusement Organization caters to the pleasure-seekers of this city. Now the great Elysium, that vast expanse of artificial ice provides healthy exercise and real happiness for thousands, during skating hours and at the National Hockey matches held there.

In summer the inimitable Euclid Beach Park is a haven from the heat. A splendid beach and every conceivable form of mechanical amusement earns for the Park unfailing patronage. **Fun there is clean, wholesome, supervised!** The Humphrey Company may be called, in truth—"Purveyors of Amusement to the People of Cleveland."

Our Summer Camp at the Beach Is Well-Equipped and Boasts Splendid Patronage.

(Illus. 24) With cap and knickers, sweater and tie, they strolled through the park or rode the AUTO TRAIN. Amid the trees we see the CARROUSEL, the GREAT AMERICAN RACING DERBY, RED BUG BOULEVARD and the SCENIC RAILWAY entrance.

(Robert Callaghan Collection)

(Illus. 25) The popularity of the AUTO TRAIN and its leisurely pace were indicative of relaxed atmosphere that pervaded much of Euclid Beach. These two views show the trai wending its way through the CAMPGROUNDS.

(Kekic Collection)

(Illus. 26) With the development of aviation and the Humphrey's interest in flying, evidence of the airplane began to appear at the Park. This early LINK TRAINER was near the entrance to the Park from the MAIN PARKING LOT. The POST OFFICE, BUG, and AEROPLANES are in the background.

(Robert Callaghan Collection)

(Illus. 27) A children's beauty contest in the '20s. The proud parents wait for a decision. The LOG CABIN can be seen in the background.

(Robert Callaghan Collection)

JUNE 8, 1924.   CLEVELAND PLAIN DEALER CONVENTION NUMBER   PAGE THIRTEEN

EUCLID BEACH PARK

THE MOST COMPLETE RECREATION AMUSEMENT PARK IN THE WORLD

By DUDLEY S. HUMPHREY

MUCH NEW AND EVERYTHING BETTER, BIGGER AND FINER AT EUCLID BEACH PARK FOR SEASON OF 1924.

THE HUMPHREY COMPANY

HALLOWEEN BRAWL

avors Open Piling Piers to Make Sand Beaches

ner of Euclid Beach Writes of lan's Success

BY D. S. HUMPHREY.

AT EUCLID BEACH NEAR THE LONG PIER.

Predicts Gord Park Will Ha Fine Shore.

23   (Illus. 28)

(Illus. 31) Try your skill with the rifle. Although there was a conspicuous absence of large numbers of "chance" games, a SHOOTING GALLERY could be found at the Beach through most of its history.

(Illus. 30) A stroll on the pier was a must if you visited the Beach. THE FOUNTAIN had not yet been installed in the circular pool as of this time. (Late '20s.)

(Illus. 29) D. S. Humphrey and the hero of the silver screen, Rin Tin Tin.

August 31, 1936

(Illus. 32)

They're in the Passing Show!

Intimate Pictures of Greater Cleveland Life Flashed Into the Record by News Cameraman

ON this Euclid Beach outing were (left to right): Jeanne Buettner, 17220 Maplebboro rd.; Millicent Randall, 13520 Superior rd.; Marge Heustein, 1757 Rosedale, and Margaret Buettner.

THE horse trough! There aren't many left in these days of horseless carriages but the few seem to get enough use to justify their retention. This Old Dobbin is gratefully drinking from a basin set next to the pavement at Kenilworth ave. and W. 14th st. in front of Lincoln park.

A LOT of steaks—and did they tantalize the nostrils! It takes a skilled workman to handle them in this fashion, but Bill Rennert (left) and Joe Angelo of Allendorf's restaurant proved they were adept at the task. The scene is back of Cleveland college and the steaks were for guests at a banquet.

[News Staff Photographer]

HAS an audience. Vincent Robatin, 14, of 9314 Kennedy ave., a student at St. Stanislaus school, is carving wood at the playground exhibit at the exposition.

THE CLEVELAND PRESS

AUG. 6, 1936

Long Lines Formed Quickly Today as Families Gathered for Press Beach Picnic

A long line for a fast ride, snapped as Press families gathered at Euclid Beach today for their annual outing.

Coming down hill on the Aero-dips, one of the rides thrown open to picnic visitors.

Arriving, left to right: Mrs. William Kish, 3412 E. 116th street; Mrs. Joseph Kish, 11405 Melba avenue; Mrs. John Thomas, 2645 E. 11th street; front, Jeanette Kish, 3; Joe Kish, 9; Dolores Kish, 7, and Bernice Thomas, 5.

Skating Sailorettes on Parade

Sailorettes, parading the width of the Elysium rink, formed one of the spectacular skating routines junior members of the Elysium Figure Skating Club presented in their part of the club's first festival last night.

The sailorettes were characters in a pageant of dolls in a toy-maker's dream, in which 300 boys and girls performed. Ninety adults appeared in the second half of the show.

And Dolls They Were

Dolls they were, indeed. Most of the children were making their first appearance before a large audience, and many of them were performing after only one season on figure skates.

Their circles were wobbly, sometimes, and their glides precarious, but their spins jumps and spread eagles gave a strong hint that Cleveland more than ever before is destined to be a formidable city in figure skating competitions to come.

Mary Jean Sturrock was a graceful little fairy doll who skated with Dr. Tuckerman to open the show.

Then came baby dolls and Teddy bears who formed a large circle from which each tiny skater performed in his specialty in turn, either alone or in a pair.

In the pageant of dolls Patty Deuring skated as a spirited Irish miss, jigging on her toes and doing the splits to steal a little more than her share of the applause.

John Tuckerman and Lois Dunkel put on a finished demonstration of junior skating as Russian dolls, and Rose Marie Hess, appearing as a Susy-Q-ing Indian, and Harriet Matson, a Swedish doll, were well applauded.

Two Sister Teams

There were two sister teams Barbara and Ella Eloy performed in a Dutch dance, and Marie and Stephanie Rinicella skated a tango.

Geraldine Nuhfer, Cleveland's fifteen-year-old North American junior speed skating champion, did a sailor's hornpipe in a court of sailors and showed she was as much at ease on the rounded runners of figure skates as her speed blades.

In the wedding scene Suzanne Ukula, daughter of Sandy Rivchun, as matron of honor and best man, surprised the crowd with acrobatics, Sandy whirling his partner free of the ice with a hand and skate hold.

M SKATERS IN CARNIVAL

iors and 90 Adults
2,500 in Audience

By DAVID J. RIMMEL

...over the ice for the last...he carnival, the seniors...s a group tango, ten-step...

...spectacular and grace...ion skating the Ukulas...Scott, assistant profes...Paul Pavlinka gave a...he skill which made him...western junior champion...ted States last year...ch Caine as premier...a ballet of blue-and-sil...alaces performed in...e was injected with...

...iors, however, who...r-die spirit to the carni...rrow escapes were fre-

25

Tomorrow

The first moving picture theater in Cleveland burned to the ground 30 years ago today. A Fourth of July crowd was at Euclid Beach in the afternoon and the World Theater there was crowded when the blaze was discovered at one side of the stage and screen. Ushers calmed the hundreds of patrons, who hurried out without panic or injury. Joseph Baldwin, a survivor of the Collinwood School fire, was one of the ushers and heroically helped direct the throng to safety. Within twenty minutes the theater was in ruins. Defective wiring was blamed for the $15,000 blaze. A tent was up the next day for continuation of the movie showings on the Monday celebrated as a holiday.

CLEVELAND, THURSDAY, JUNE 1, 1939   Press   Entered as sec...Post Office...

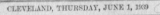

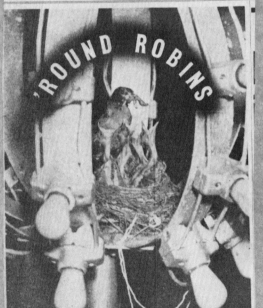

Photographer James Meli opens his lens just as the birdies enjoy their lunch

4 Tiny Robins, Robbin' Rides, Happy Atop Merry-Go-Round

By GEORGE DAVIS

Life is a whirl to this robin family, for their nest is under the cupola of a merry-go-round at Euclid Beach Park. Around and around and around they go, and where they will stop they never know.

...Dick Shean picked the spot...make liked it, for the merry-go-round is smack over the open sides of the park section called Kiddieland.

"That," she said, "is the place to get. I can set in the rain and never get wet."

Four young robins hatched out several days before this part of the park opened for the summer. Then the merry-go-round started, Mamma Robin was alarmed when the yellow bulbs all around the nest were turned on. But the four young robins were delighted.

"Hi!" yelled the little birds. "Ain't this fast. We'll ride and ride till the day is done. Papa ain't asked to pay the rent, and all our rides don't cost a cent."

Mamma Robin waits until the...

...the snaileworms she gathers on lawns in the park. This chore is shared by Cock Robin.

Phil White, teacher at Garfield Heights High, directs Kiddieland. He guesses the four little robins think all nests revolve like the one in which they were hatched. That notion is shared by the assistant park manager, J. E. Lembo Jr.

John Saxton, master mechanic, remembers there was a robin nest in the same spot three years ago. Cock Robin is one of that breed, he thinks. Revolving in the merry-go-round got his directions mixed, and it took him two years to find his way back, says Mr. Saxton.

The four little robins, in their revolving nest, are getting a musical education listening to organs of several carrousels. A tune they hear so...

MONDAY, JUNE 5, 1939

Catholic Children Drop Books for P...

All set for schools' picnic

Children from all the Catholic schools in Greater Cleveland laid aside their school books today and gathered at Euclid Beach Park for their annual picnic. On the program were races, games, rides and traditional picnic "eats." Shown above are children from St. Anthony's...dren from St. Anthony's, access...by a nun, they arrived...park.

Young Pass... at Sleepy Know 'Casey

"Sure all the child...I have hauled as ma...one day," said Mike N...St. Clair Avenue N. f...the Sleepy Hollow Ra...clid Beach, yesterday...

It may be a min...but Mike is no min...for in 1892 he start...fireman on the We...Railroad and in 1898...engineer.

In 1925 he was f...neer on the Sleep...engine, though, and...1904 and runs exac...engines that he use...takes the same grip...tive that he did in...

He carefully oils...it pulls into the...three-quarter-mile...sure that the m...keep the track in...

In three...

(Illus. 33) A young shuffleboard player a la nickers. This area of the park was especially pleasant at night; there was soft lighting and sounds from the dance bands on one side with lapping waves on the other. All was intermingled with the ambience of the rides and people in the background.

(Illus. 34) "They also 'anticipate' who stand" in line. The THRILLER was always one of the most popular rides in the park. Here, in the '20s we see riders waiting their turn.

(Robert Callaghan Collection)

(Illus. 35) Just glad to be there; Wouldn't we all? This family in the '30s is seen near the SHUFFLEBOARD courts that were located on the lake-side of the DANCE PAVILION. (This was formerly an outdoor dance floor.)

(Russell Allon Hehr Collection

So much time has been spent waiting for things to pass, such as the depression and World War II, that often the value of what we have or had is ignored.

We waited for peace, then more sophisticated entertainment; peace was not appreciated and new forms of recreation were disappointing. Meanwhile the Beach began to drift out of existence.

(Illus. 36) Those who remember the park well know that this route of entrance from the MAIN PARKING LOT was the beginning of a visit to this special place called EUCLID BEACH.

(Richman Bros.)

29

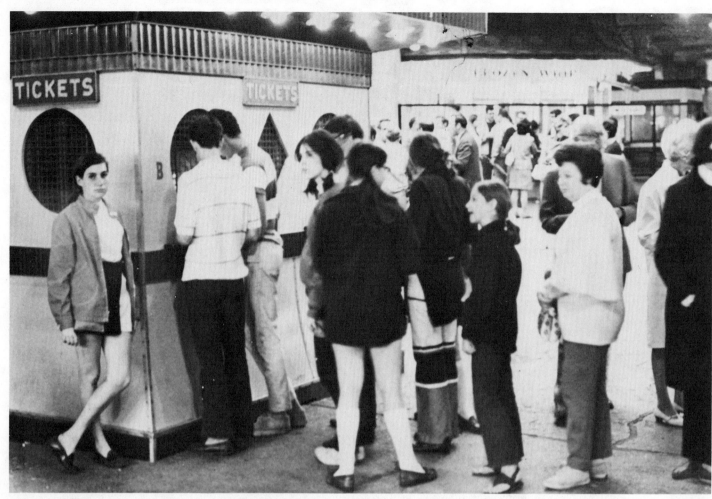

(Illus. 37) Although styles changed the gathering of tickets to get to the fun and the goodies was perennial at Euclid Beach.

(The Humphrey Company)

(Illus. 38) Saddle shoes, "bobby sox", Bermuda shorts and "pegged" pants were the order of the day. (July, 1958). Looking eastward the GREAT AMERICAN RACING DERBY building is on the left, the FLYING TURNS facade is on the right.

31   (Neva Hansen)

(Illus. 39) The look of the '50s. These young girls "await" their weight.
(Russell Allon Hehr Collection)

(Illus. 40, 40a, 40b, 40c, 40d, 40e, 40f) Some came just to play miniature golf in the 1950s. They would know each and every bump and pitch of the playing surface of each hole. The course was lit by soft yellow lights and the sound of the Artizan Band organ at the ROCKET SHIPS filled the air.

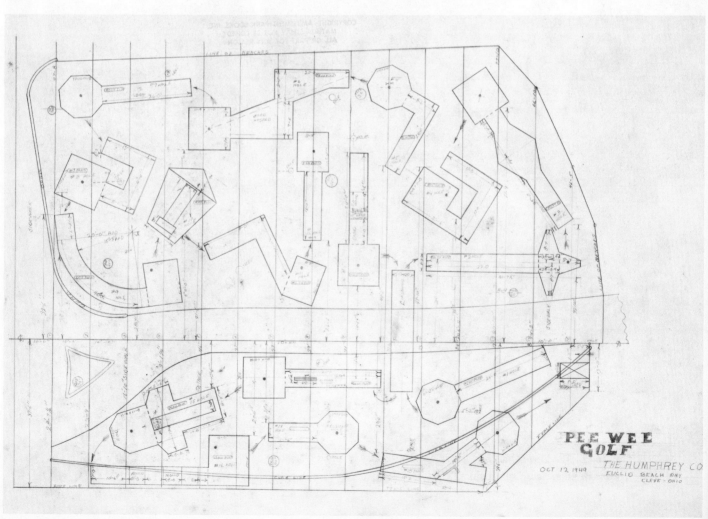

(Illus. 41)

(Illus. 40a)

(Illus. 40b)

(Illus. 40c)

(Illus. 40d)

(Illus. 40e)

(Illus. 40f)

(William Stoneback Collection)

(Illus. 4

The Clevela

EUCLID BEACH CAMP →

June 30 1950 Plain Dealer

EUCLID BEACH
5...

Stock check-up: Bernie Hones (left) and George Schaub.

T. J. Harrold pours lemonade for (left to right) Mrs. W. H. Benham, Mrs. Harrold and W. H. Benham.

Folks at Home

Fresh from the shower: Charles S. Lawson.

Mrs. Blanche Hunt (left) gives morning mail to Mrs. Donald Alexander

Off to the laundry: Linda Wilson, 3, and Mrs. William Wilson.

Water girls: Mrs. Dan Miller; Pamela Ann Miller, 5 months; Sheryl Kae Bider, 10.

Thousands still can recall the splashing thrills on the old Mill Chute.

Streetcars once looped into park where concrete pavilion now stands.

By MARIE DAERR

Along about March, a certain group of people in Cleveland apartments and furnished rooms, in Florida hotels and tourist homes, find their thoughts returning to a colony of tent cottages on streets named Magnolia, Viola, Virginia, Cumberland.

They are the summer-long residents of Euclid Beach Park Camp, a congenial band which adjusts happily to the echo of delighted shrieks from the Thriller and Flying Turns and which feels deep pity for anyone who must spend the hot months "in town."

For some 35 cottage-tent families like the W. H. Benhams, 12-year veterans, spending May 1 to Oct. 1 at the beach entails shrugging off such departures from routine as drawing water from an outdoor faucet, donning bathrobe and slippers for a stroll to the showers and, if they prefer doing their own weekly wash, sharing a well-equipped community laundry.

For 14 other families, for whom the camp season extends until Nov. 1, life's a bit more citified. They're folks like the Donald Alexanders, who have spent 29 years at 39 Magnolia Dr., in a stucco cottage equipped with running water, toilet and shower, and made luxurious by the Alexanders' own deep-piled rugs, upholstered furniture and thriving house plants.

Camp Is Friendly

For retired T. J. Harrold and Mrs. Harrold, who celebrated their Golden Wedding anniversary at the beach Aug. 14, 1948, the camp offers a chance to chat with friends they have made during 15 summers, to sit in deck chairs in the sun, to putter with the coxcomb in their tiny front garden. Next door to the Harrolds lives their daughter, Mrs. Elizabeth Stelter, a camp resident since 1932.

"Coming here after a winter in an apartment gives us a wonderful lift," said Harrold. "Why, I don't know how people stand the heat in the city. It must be five to 10 degrees cooler out here."

For Charles S. Lawson, who has an after-dark shift with Yellow Cab, and for William Wilson, a night switchman for New York Central Railroad, a summer at the beach means "a vacation while working."

Like other cottage-tent dwellers, the Wilsons, parents of three-year-old Linda, have supplemented their summer home's furnishings with possessions of their own. They brought linens, lamps, dishes, Mrs. Wilson's sewing machine, Linda's crib and toys.

Regulars Sing Praises of Euclid Beach Camp

And, like others at the camp, the Wilsons have relatives nearby. Next door are Wilson's brother, Richard, a New York Central brakeman, with his wife and 10-month-old daughter, Shirley.

Also summering at the camp are another brother and his wife, Mr. and Mrs. Lloyd Wilson. Wilson is one of a number of tent residents who work at Euclid Beach Park. He manages four rides.

Cousin Is Baby-Sitter

The Dan Millers, married in November, 1948, spent the summer of 1949 at Euclid Beach. This season, five-month-old Pamela Ann is a resident of 13 Viola Ave. Enthusiastic baby-sitter for Pam is her visiting cousin, 10-year-old Sheryl Kae Bider of Manistee, Mich.

"You couldn't ask for a nicer vacation spot," said Mrs. Miller. "I feel so safe here. If a stranger appears, the park guards are there in a minute. My only problem is keeping friendly squirrels from climbing into the baby buggy to take a peek at Pam."

Seven-year-old Karen Eddy and her brother, Thomas, 10, who live with their parents, Mr. and Mrs. Byron A. Eddy, at 35 Cumberland, have grown up on summers at Euclid Beach.

"We first brought Thomas to the camp when he was a baby," said Mrs. Eddy. "We start our season before school vacation begins. Karen and Thomas take the bus from here to Memorial School.

"My parents, the Thomas Taylors, are spending their 17th summer at 10 Poplar Ave. My grandmother used to come here, too, years ago."

At the Eddy cottage, a television set is among furnishings of the screened parlor-porch, most important room of any Euclid Beach summer residence. The M. F. Thunhursts' porch, in Chinese red, holds travel souvenirs and an old-fashioned, cane-seated rocker which Mrs. Thunhurst finds indispensable to her summer contentment. The Thunhursts will leave Oct. 15 for Hollywood, Fla.

Mrs. Ada Wolf, who also winters in Florida, pointed out the cabinet, discarded by its former owner, which she spruced up with paint for summer use in her Surrey Lane tent-cottage. Mrs. Wolf's son, Eugene, comes home each afternoon from nearby Eaton Manufacturing, where he is a chemist, to enjoy canoeing, swimming, dancing. During the winter, he has an apartment "in the city."

Mention Euclid Beach Park to the campers and the response is an amused grin.

"People who describe the camp as 'that noisy place' don't know what they're talking about," scoffed stucco-dweller Mrs. Alexander. "It's only once in a while, when the wind's blowing from that direction, that I hear the people on the Thriller."

"When the sound from the park stops, you wonder what's happened," said Mrs. John Comerford, who lives nearer the amusement park, at 24 Virginia Ave. Mrs. Comerford, a camper since 1924, is the mother of Patricia Jane, 15, and Nettie Claire, 13, junior life guards at the park pool.

"The sounds from the park lull me to sleep," chuckled Mrs. Dick Tuschong, 30 years at the beach.

38 Years at Beach

Reminiscences come easily to Mr. and Mrs. William G. Sharp, who, after spending 38 summers at the beach, have substituted less strenuous pleasures for the dancing, bowling, tennis and boating they used to enjoy; the L. W. Youngs, who recall the prewar parties the summer people held every two weeks, and Mr. and Mrs. Walter Evans, who showed a snapshot of the log cabin, now torn down, in which they used to summer at the beach.

Milk, baked goods, dry cleaning, diapers and other laundry are delivered to camp residents. The summer people pick up their mail at the camp office, where J. A. Anderson is manager and Mrs. Blanche Hunt is rental clerk.

Marketing is done at Bernie Hones' grocery, situated at the camp site for 22 years and for the past 14 managed by George Schaub, who spends the winter working at a grocery store in Miami.

Hones is year-round proprietor of another store, just west of Euclid Beach at 15555 Lake Shore Blvd. A twin brother Garry; a sister, Mrs. Bernadine Kramer, and a niece, Miss Gertrude Holkenburg, are in business with him.

During the summer, Bernie Hones, his sister and niece share a Euclid Beach summer residence at 31 Lincoln Dr., while Schaub occupies a cottage at 18 Viola Ave.

35

CLOTHES HORSES

HALTER WESKIT OF WHITE PIQUE (left) gets a scattering of navy blue polka dots to match cotton shorts. Weskit also comes in black and white, costs $5. Shorts, also available in red and china blue, cost $4.50. Navy blue cotton (right) makes the boned strapless top that ties with a sash at the waist, $7.95. Bermuda shorts come in navy or sky blue, red and white, cost $4.50.

(Press photos by Glen Zahn at Euclid Beach Park)

CRAZY PANTS ARE COPIED from a court jester and are made of black and white striped cotton chintz. Slim and straight, they're tied at the knee, cost $5.95. Cotton broadcloth shirt comes in white, red and ice blue, costs $7.95.

A MAYLAYAN PRINT'S GAY COLORS sparkle on the charcoal gray background of Madalyn Miller's halter-topped cotton sundress. The full skirt swirls in the breezes, price is $17.95. Engel-Fetzer clothes are modeled by members of the Cain Park Theater cast opening in the production of "Carousel" Monday.

The Press Women's Pages

Edited by Jane Olds   Wednesday, July 1, 1953

By ELIZABETH LUFT

An afternoon at the park or picnicking in the country are happy ways to spend a bright summer's day, particularly if there are children in the family.

Don gay sports clothes, preferably of sturdy material, and then give yourself over to having fun. Denim, pique, chambray and colorfully-printed cotton have been styled to please for every figure and taste.

Tops on the list are separates composed of blouses and skirts for cover up to and from your vacation spot. Underneath, a strip tease reveals halter and shorts to give you attractive exposure for a tan and cool breezes.

Fancy pants in stripes, prints and bright colors team with blouses or halter tops, pedal pushers are combined with a turtle-neck sweater for a cool day.

(Illus. 44) The time is July, 1959 and the place is the CARROUSEL at Euclid Beach Park. This grand machine was brought to the park in 1910 and was a product of the Philadelphia Toboggan Company.

(Illus. 45) "Just hangin' around the old CARROUSEL". The classic merry-go-round as it appeared in 1959.

(Illus. 46) Park benches built around the trees, the CIGAR STAND, with the CARROUSEL in the distance were familiar to visitors in the 1950s.

(Neva Hansen)

Reference to this map of Cleveland streets will show you the best and most convenient route to Euclid Beach Park from any point in the city.

SERVICE CHART
CLEVELAND AND VICINITY

© 1935 BY Kardpak – BEREA, OHIO

SCALE OF MILES

EUCLID BEACH PARK

ERIE

LAKE

LAKEWOOD

★ EUCLID BEACH

WORLD'S
FINEST
PARK

On
Lake Erie
in Cleveland

Owned and Operated
for 38 Years by

The HUMPHREY
COMPANY

A WORLD OF FUN FOR EVERYONE

Bathing

Half a mile of wide beach—and a pool with clean running water. Lifeguards insure constant protection and safety.

oating

arge battery of row boats available; and king facilities for yachts and small craft.

Fishing

Right from the pier, or from boats. Tackle, Bait and Boats always available.

Restaurant and Cafeteria

Large and well appointed dining rooms right on the lake. A perfect spot from which to watch the beautiful sunset. Good, pure foods moderately priced.

uto Train

't miss a ride through the Park on this sual train—the same train that conted visitors through the grounds of the ama-Pacific Exposition in California.

(Illus. 47)   (The Humphrey Company)

TAKEN FOR A RIDE

Rides are the principal ingredients of an amusement park. Their profiles, features, colors and every sound and smell will be major contributions to what a park will become. Euclid Beach Park had roller coasters, carrousels, dark rides, ferris wheels, and the like. The real difference between Euclid Beach and most other parks was the harmony among the rides, trees and other elements located on those acres. It seemed each ride had its own qualities and yet was inextricably blended with every other element on the grounds.

The rides themselves were not randomly placed, but yet not regimented in some over-obvious scheme. From the FLYING TURNS to the BUG, from the RACING COASTER to KIDDIE-LAND and from the GREAT AMERICAN RACING DERBY to OVER THE FALLS, there was a uniquely special countenance that was EUCLID BEACH PARK.

(Illus. 48) Climbing the 71'5" first hill of the THRILLER. The fronts of the cars were open so all the action was visible. At this stage of the ride seasoned passengers knew a good ride was in store; the neophyte was in for a few surprises. Up, up and . . .

(Donald Ressler Collection)

(Illus. 50)

(Illus. 50, 51) The SCOOTER was always a popular ride that gave a rider the opportunity to determine some of the action of the ride.

(Tom Satyrshur Collection)

(Illus. 51)

(Illus. 49) The FLYING SCOOTER was a product of the Bisch-Rocco firm of Chicago and was brought to Euclid Beach in 1938.

(Tom Satyrshur Collection)

41

(Illus. 52) During the latter decades of the park's operation most
visitors came there by car. Upon entering the park from the MAIN
PARKING LOT the FLYING SCOOTERS (now often called "Butter-
flys") was one of the first rides to be seen. This popular ride that gave
the rider an element of control. "Snap those cables as you try to clear
the COLONNADE."

(Robert Callaghan Collection)

(Illus. 53) Detail of the decor (not the ladies) is evident in this close up
of a FLYING SCOOTERS car. Maintenance of rides and attention to
detail made Euclid Beach a leader in safety and cleanliness.

(Neva Hansen)

(Russell Allon Hehr Collection)

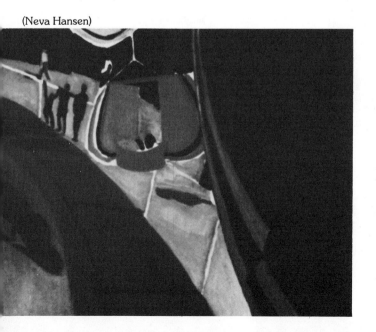

(Illus. 55) Many of those waiting to get on the BUG were "flappers." With their beaus in straw hats, all partook in the roar of the '20s. The painting scheme on the ride cars seems to reflect a little of World War I aircraft marking. The BUG was always popular. It was a ride where you could literally rub elbows with others.

(Robert Callaghan Collection)

(Illus. 56) The BUG offered a real togetherness in riding. As the riders were tossed forward and back the fun and laughs increased.

(Richman Bros.)

(Richman Bros.)   (Illus. 57)

(Illus. 58)

(Illus. 57) As was the FLYING SCOOTERS, the BUG was near the
MAIN PARKING LOT entrance and was one of the initial rides seen
upon coming into the park. It also had a significant sound, a sort of
buzzing due to the chain mechanism.

(Illus. 58) The BUG, happy visitors and tree shaded walkways. Remember? Harmony between manmade excitement and nature was
a hallmark of the Beach.

(Russell Allon Hehr Collection)   (Illus. 60)

(Harry Luikart Collection)   (Illus. 61)   (Harry Luikart Collection)   (Illus. 62)

(Illus. 59)

(Richman Bros.)

(Illus. 59, 63) Two views of the ROCKET SHIPS. Riders from the Richman picnic await blast-off, and then enjoy the ride through that special space.

(Illus. 60) It was almost serene as the gleaming ROCKET SHIPS floated through the trees amid the breezes of the lake, accompanied by the lilting band organ melodies.

(Illus. 61) A product of the Traver Engineering Company and originally called the CIRCLE SWING, the ROCKET SHIPS endured until the end in 1969. The cars were changed three times from gondolas to biplanes and finally to the "Buck Rogers" inspired ROCKET SHIPS.

(Illus. 62) The ships themselves were Humphrey Company products, designed, produced and unique to the Beach. Larger than examples found at any other traditional parks which copied those at the Beach they were yet another hallmark of the park's character.

(Richman Bros.)   (Illus. 63)

(Illus. 64) A sunny afternoon in the '20s, all of your family and/or your best girl or guy, a straw hat and new chapeau (ladies' headware) plus a ride on the AEROPLANES. . . . Who could ask for anything more! Can you hear the Artizan band organ playing under the rush of air caused by the ride? (Goodrich Picnic)

(Robert Callaghan Collection)

AEROPLANES

2 TICKETS   2 TICKETS

(Illus. 65) The MILL CHUTE was installed in 1921 by the Philadelphia Toboggan Company. The OVER-THE-FALLS was completed in 1938 and was actually a redesigning of the MILL CHUTE. "Hold onto your hats" was a sign displayed on many of the rides. Here someone takes that advice.

(William Stoneback Collection)

(Illus. 66) A boat load of riders about to enter the tunnel of the OVER-THE-FALLS. Quietly, the boat would glide through the dark channel until mounting the 35 hill and the subsequent "fall".

(Robert Callaghan Collection)

(Illus. 67) Boat meets water Splashing Fun! The old MILL CHUTE with its dark tunnel offered people of the day a chance for intimacy before the plunge. The SCENIC RAILWAY is on the left.

50

(Illus. 68) Above. Eager riders board the waiting boat at the loading platform of OVER-THE-FALLS.

(Illus. 69) Below. The boat has entered the darkened channel and a new group of passengers wait for the next boat. Some would-be passengers might have had second thoughts as they watched drenched riders disembark from the boat they themselves were about to board.

(Illus. 70) Above. More cause for hesitancy was the view of the seeming vertical drop (actually 35°) of the OVER-THE-FALLS hill.

(Illus. 71) Below. "Calm water at last!" The boat stopped pitching and soon the crew of this plunging voyage could adjourn to the POP CORN STAND and wring out their hair.

Beac

(Illus. 73) RED BUG BOULEVARD was a reflection of interest in the automobile. Its roadway of solid maple wound in and out of the RACING COASTER structure. Here, some youths of the '20s are seen near the entrance which was next to that of the SCENIC RAILWAY. "Gee Mom, can I go on again?"

(Illus. 72) This picture shows the RED BUG cars in detail. Later, fronts were affixed to the cars so ladies could drive in a more modest fashion. The entrance ramp to the SCENIC RAILWAY is on the left. The '20s were still "roaring".

(Illus. 74) The carved horse, the painted pony, the carrousel were basic to the amusement park and youth. This young girl clutches the neck of one of the FLYING PONIES. The ride was installed in the park in 1903 and remained until 1938.

(Russell Allon Hehr Collection)

(Illus. 75) These four youngster are in the outdoor WHIP which was adjacent to the SCENIC RAIL WAY. This ride was a product o W. F. Mangels.

(Russell Allon Hehr Collection)

(Amusement Park Books, Inc.)

(Illus. 76) Floating in the night: the grand CARROUSEL. The Philadelphia Toboggan classic of 1910, stayed through the park's last season. Remember your equestrian fantasies?

(Illus. 77) Severe Art Deco designs were painted on the inner and outer panels of the CARROUSEL in the '30s, militating against the curves and Baroque feeling of the original.

(Harry Luikart Collection)

(Illus. 78, 79) The magnificant chariots on the CARROUSEL. These works were a mark of grandeur from Philadelphia Toboggan carvers.

(William Stoneback Collection)

(Illus. 80, 81, 82) Three views insde the GREAT AMERICAN RACING DERBY. This unique ride featured four abreast racing horses. At one time in its operation, the winning horse's rider was entitled to another ride, free. This was designated by the placement of a small American flag on the head of the carved horse.

(Illus. 81)

(Norm Worgull Collection)

n Satyrshur Collection)

(Illus. 82)

(Illus. 83) Inside the grand CARROUSEL. The white horses and typical Philadelphia Toboggan Co. construction are only marred by the inapproprate art deco designs.

58

(Illus. 85) Did they win? "What a great ride." Everybody really won. This happy train load of people just completed the course. (1950s)

(Illus. 86) Negotiating the turnaround above the station the RACING COASTER trains head back towards Lakeshore Blvd. and the final leg of the competition.

(Illus. 87) The facade of the RACING COASTER shows another Art Deco feature which was applied in the 1930s.

(Harry Luikart Collection)

(Illus. 84) The brilliant coaster designer John Miller, conceived the RACING COASTER for the Beach in 1913. This aerial view shows the entire course. The plan reveals that there was only really one tract arranged in parallel fashion. One may remember boarding on one side of the platform and disembarking on the other. Maybe you had too much fun to care about such things?

(Harry Luikart Collection)

(Illus. 88) This later picture of the RACING COASTER shows the infield sans RED BUG. It also exemplifies the "stacked" design of the structure, one series of dips on top of the other.

(Illus. 89) A later photo of the RACING COASTER reveals the FLYING TURNS on the right and the redesigned water ride, the OVER-THE-FALLS, near the vacant former site of the SCENIC RAILWAY on the left. The RED BUG BOULEVARD is still present.

(Richman Bros.)

(Robert Callaghan Collection)

(Illus. 89a) With the SCENIC RAILWAY on the left and the THRILLER on the right, the RACING COASTER occupies the center of coaster activity. The THRILLER train is seen topping the higher second hill which was originally constructed in 1924. This hill was sharply reduced in height soon after the initial season. The FLYING TURNS was just a dream at the time of this picture. (1924)

3506

(Illus. 90) The ride attendants timed the release of each of the RACING COASTER trains so the competition was fair or as fair as possible. The lattice work inside the loading station is of the style of amusement park architecture in the early part of the 20th century.

LEFT: The tug of war. The tenors on the left won from the basses.

BELOW: Wheelbarrow race. Running: J. A. McMahon, Cleveland Law Director J. P. Lamb, E. A. Kraft, E. L. Bottle, H. M. Dunham. On hands: George Anderson, E. J. Tyler, E.W. Lehr, Z. A. Moss, J. V. Miller.

Plain Dealer Photo.

BELOW: The "Fifty-Fifty" sentiment frequently was exemplified by Cleveland orphans at their annual picnic.

WHEN CLEVELAND ORPHANS enjoyed their annual picnic at Euclid Beach under auspices of the Cleveland Automobile Club, the children had individual attention and the little fellow at the left seemed flabbergasted by it all. The youngsters had tickets for everything that the park afforded, but the Derby Racer, pictured below, was one of the most popular attractions. Grown-ups accompanied the children and they, too, seemed to enjoy the rides.

Plain Dealer Photo.

OURSE members of the Automobile Club had to ride on the merry-nd. It wouldn't be fair to the orphans to play all day with them at Beach and then fail them at such a time. Then, too, the orphans ng the picnic might fall off. Anyway, there were lots of twosomes "flying horses."

And how the sun shone on the first Sunday of the season—

It made the tulip bed which you see up in the corner a blazing riot of color

The little cry of two thousand who live on ten tents were glad to see it

Brief Subjects on Euclid Beach Park

(Doris Humphrey)

The Speed of the Roller Coasters

The speed of the coaster rides when you are on them, racing around turns and up and down hills, seems to be at fifty or sixty miles per hour. The Flying Turns actually averages no more than twenty-seven miles per hour and the Thriller about thirty. In order to determine the speed of a ride, two lines are drawn on the track exactly fifty feet apart; the timer holds a stop-watch that makes one revolution in three seconds; he stands where he can see the starting and finish lines and gets an accurate timing on the fifty feet; from that the average speed in miles per hour is computed for the whole ride.

* * * *

The speed of a ride varies quite a little, depending on various conditions. The more heavily a train is loaded the faster it will go. Also the warmer the evening the faster the ride.

* * * *

When the Thriller was first built, several of us made loud and disparaging complaints that, with all the time and energy and money that had been expended, the ride was far from good enough. It was slow. And, being slow the cars failed to give the customers that feeling of flying through space, of being very light, and of floating over the tops of the hills.

Then, one day, a small delegation of old and constant patrons of the park walked into the office and told Mr. Humphrey that they had been riding on the Thriller and thought he ought to know that it was almost throwing the customers right out of the seats. Mr. Humphrey straightway investigated. He found that the ride had spontaneously increased its speed. In fact, it had increased its speed too much. To be absolutely safe it had to be slowed down. The great jump in speed had come on a Saturday night. Early the next morning, all the carpenters and ride men gathered together and before opening time raised the track at the bottom of the first dip in order to slow the speed of the ride down to where it did not toss the patrons up and down quite so freely but still gave them all the necessary thrills.

It always takes time for the track on any ride to attain its fastest and smoothest surface.

* * * *

The Roller Rink

If you count the number of years in the lives of most of the roller rinks that you have known, you will find that very few of them have ever lived to be more than three years of age. The first year the floor is smooth and the skates are grand. The next year the skates begin to get pretty wobbly. The third year the floor gets rough and the skates become simply impossible. The fourth year the people become disgusted with the generally run-down state of the place and allow it to slide into bankruptcy.

The roller rink at the Beach has been in thriving existence since 1902 —because every year the floor is gone over and three times each year the skates are repaired.

Refreshments, Suppers, and Lunches at Euclid Beach

A patron of the park was carrying on some business in a wholesale meat market. In the course of his call there, he says, he learned something about the Beach that he approved of very highly.

He and the owner had been chatting and walking around the market. As they passed a large ice-box filled with wieners, the visitor asked. "Where do all of those go?"

"Out to the Beach to be hot dogs," was the reply. "We keep them separate because they're specials. Higher quality meat than in the average grade."

The standards designated in this little episode are maintained in connection with all other foods that are sold in the park. In several places throughout the grounds, either under the cover of buildings or outside under the trees, there are long rows of picnic tables for those who wish to patronize the near-by lunch stands that are known for their good coffee, toasted sandwiches, pie, ice-cream, and soft drinks, or for those who have brought their own picnic lunches.

Observation Post

(By Amelia Donahue)

I find while enjoying a walk through the park
A popular ride called the "Laff-in-the-Dark,"
Just get yourself set for a pleasant surprise:
It's a great deal more than the title implies.

The "Flying Turns" spins out as many sharp thrills
As the near-by "Thriller" with its breath-taking hills;
Then the "Dodgem" — so full of bumps and of fun;
The "Great Racing Derby"—Look, my horse has won!

"The Surprise House" seemed most intriguing to me—
So clever and cunning and cute as could be.
In all of the corners, surprises galore;
When you reach the end, you will wish there were more.

Now on through the park to the numerous rides—
The "Bug" and the "Scenic" with the dips, curves and dives
And then on the "Auto Train" we ride away
Quite happy to have had so pleasant a day.

Then back from our ride, and on a bench near-by,
I prepare to go when my wandering eye
Catches flashes of color — bright beams of light.
Then soft strains of music float out through the night.

With a glad little cry I hurry away,
So anxious to hear Austin Wylie's Band play.
While dancing the "Moonlight" I say in the dark
"A perfect finish for my day at the park."

Class C

(Doris

Various cham
Euclid Beach
Sunday. Riley,
baseman a sa
sessed, had to b
has taken on
working on S
from the outfi
responsibilities
a grand all-ar
Kohal filled th
position. Star
second for the
and still anothe
the 7th inning
is very willing
does it equall
taken off third
ter while Bo
over the thre
changes it is
the aim for li
power has bee
Sunday's g
for Euclid Be
runs, while th
ting 3 hits an
Lake, in parti
hat. Gedeon
formidable th
The Beach ha
the help of er
lins and hits
first inning an
The 6th inni
hitting by t
shaw's sing
and Klic's su
All the w
Wendelins we
the excellenc
with very m
especially, th
by Zak in the
and to the le

63

(Illus. 92) Two trains of the RACING COASTER are in even pacing. The wooden roadway of the RED BUG BOULEVARD, with a junior driver en route, is visible.

(Robert Callaghan Collection)

BARGAIN DAY!
TUESDAY
AUGUST 19
1:00 pm till midnight
ALL RIDES 5¢
Except THRILLER 10¢, DODGEM 10¢, PONY RIDE 10¢, ROTOR 10¢

(Edward C. Chukayne Collection)

(The Humphrey Company)

(Illus. 95) A maze of structures, this elevated view shows the SCENIC RAILWAY turn-around, parts of the RACING COASTER in the foreground, the tunnel of the MILL CHUTE snaking through the structures and part of the THRILLER in the background.

(Illus. 94) The SCENIC RAILWAY was one of the earliest coasters built at the Beach. It was an L. A. Thompson ride (he is credited with developing the modern roller coaster) which was constructed in 1907 and remained until 1938. Here, picnickers play baseball on the future side of the RACING COASTER and THRILLER.

(Illus. 96) A later picture (60s) shows a train full of riders approaching the THRILLER'S first hill.

(Harry Luikart Collection)

(Illus. 97) A familiar sight, the THRILLER on the way up, you can almost hear the click and clatter of the clutch dog.

(Harry Luikart Collection)

(Illus. 98) Over the top. Note the crowning structure—the ornate style of the times.

(Robert Callaghan Collection)

(Illus. 99) Riders with suits and ties (1920s). The area where the FLYING TURNS would be constructed is on the right.

(Robert Callaghan Collection)

(Illus. 100) Up the lift on the THRILLER with the high original second hill evident (1924). The presence of hats verifies the need of the warning "Hold onto your hats!"

(Robert Callaghan Collection)

(Illus. 101) The faces tell the story. Although a classic 1920s coaster, the THRILLER remained uncommonly smooth as well as fast through its last trip. This was a credit to designer Herbert Smeck of the Philadelphia Toboggan Company and Euclid Beach maintenance.

(Illus. 102) The first hill descent of the THRILLER. This 1924 Philadelphia Toboggan coaster was a high point of any visit to the Beach. The
hill of 71'5" delivered what any coaster rider wanted.

(Illus. 104) Down the long brake run into the station. A fully loaded THRILLER train brings its passengers into the unloading area. On the right is a signal device utilizing various colored lights to inform the operator where the trains were on the course. The date is 1967 during an Addressograph-Multigraph picnic.

(Arthur Steele Collection)

(Harry Luikart Collection)

(Illus. 103, 105) Two views of the "dog-leg" turn of the THRILLER near Lakeshore Blvd.

(Illus. 106) The last of the great rides build at Euclid Beach was the exciting FLYING TURNS. Located just east of the THRILLER, this ride featured a bob-sled like barrel where free-wheeling trains ran up and down the sides of the barrel, while descending through the course.

(William Stoneback Collection)

(Illus. 107) This FLYING TURNS train enters the final portion of the course. The use of a "crowd brake" was to help slow the cars prior to entering the unloading area. Friction between brake shoes mounted on the sides of the cars and the long brake shoe or "crowd brake" which forced or crowded the trains down to the center of the barrel accomplished the slowing process during the final series of of complete turns.

(Arthur Steele Collection)

(Illus. 108) The end of the FLYING TURNS course featured a series of severely tight circles plus the opposing forces of friction and centrifugal force. It was truly a climactic point in one of the greatest rides ever devised. At the right is a train of cars hoisted in the air to either be stored or serviced. Art Steele is in the background inspecting this part of the ride.

(Illus. 109) The FLYING TURNS stood at the east end of "coaster row". The THRILLER stands at the right and beyond at the left the far ends of the THRILLER's and RACING COASTER's courses can be seen.

(Illus. 110) Young riders flying through the "TURNS". The erratic course followed by the three-car trains is evident.

(Arthur Steele Collection)

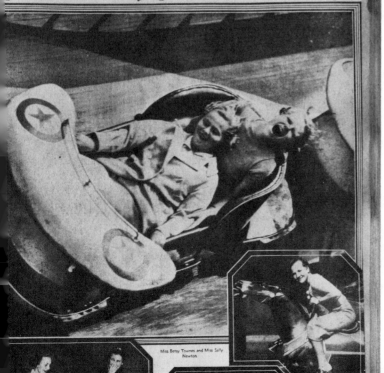

THE CLEVELAND PRESS — SEPT. 7, 1935

graduates Make "Flying Turns" Before College Opens

Miss Betsy Townes and Miss Sally Newton

(The Humphrey Company)

(Illus. 112) The WITCHING WAVES was a short-lived ride that attempted to give the sensation of a mild sort of surfing as the cars were pushed around by the metal floor which undulated like small waves. The building was soon to house the LAFF-IN-THE-DARK, utilizing the same cars.

(Illus. 113) To many a young rider the LAFF-IN-THE-DARK was terrifying. The ingenious paintings on the facade did little to dispel that fear. Here a car begins its "perilous" journey into the layout.

(Illus. 114) The DODGEM was next to the building that housed the WITCHING WAVES (later to be LAFF-IN-THE-DARK). More recently this type of ride has been called "Bumper Cars."

"Dodgem"

To D. S. Humphrey

—dean of amusement men

THE wisdom, courage and vision of D. S. Humphrey have long been an inspiration to amusement men everywhere. A staunch friend, a shrewd counselor, and a tireless worker in the interests of better and cleaner amusement parks, Mr. Humphrey richly deserves every tribute which we of the amusement world can tender him.

Mr. Humphrey's confidence in Dodgem is a matter of record. A Dodgem ride has been a prominent feature at Euclid Beach since 1921 and this Summer sixty Dodgem cars are in operation. Mr. Humphrey is especially impressed by the showing made by the new Front Wheel Drive Dodgem cars and stated recently that this year's Dodgem business gave strong indication of being bigger than ever before.

When you attend the N. A. A. P. meeting at Euclid Beach be sure to see the new Front Wheel Drive DODGEM in operation and note the wonderful popularity among Euclid Beach patrons.

DODGEM CORPORATION
706 Bay State Bldg.   Lawrence, Mass.

FRONT WHEEL DRIVE
DODGEM

(Illus. 116) A fully loaded AUTO TRAIN moves by the GREAT AMERICAN RACING DERBY.

us. 117) The AUTO TRAIN was a leisurely paced
hicle that gave its passengers a look at most of the
rk including the CAMPGROUNDS. Before the time of
e "SKYRIDE" this served as an "on-the-ground" survey
the park.

(Illus. 118)

(Illus. 118, 119) The area just northeast of the FLYING TURNS hosted a number of temporary rides. Here we see two views of the SCRAMBLER, one of those rides. (c. 1969)

(Illus. 119)

(Illus. 120) The TILT-A-WHIRL and FERRIS WHEEL occupied the area where the GREAT AMERICAN RACING DERBY once stood.

(Illus. 121) The TURNPIKE was one of the later rides to be installed at the Beach. Here, one of the cars goes under the bridge which still stands near the high-rise apartments located on the old Euclid Beach acreage.

(Illus. 122) The ROTOR was a popular ride which appeared in the last decade. It replaced the BUBBLE BOUNCE. One paid as many tickets to watch as one did to ride.

(Illus. 123) The ANTIQUE CARS took over the ROLLER RINK for the last few seasons of the Park's operation.

(Parmadale Collection)

(Russell Allon Hehr Collection

(Illus. 124) The SWINGIN GYM was a later attraction that had a short stay at the park. It was moved by the muscle power of its riders.

(Ben and Esther Schreibman Collection)
(Artist Sculptor; Karl Vidstrand, California)

(Illus. 125) With no admission charge, riding required the purchase of tickets at one of these familiar booths. The CARROUSEL is in the background.

(Harry Luikart Collection)

A LAND FOR KIDDIES

Visions of the old amusement parks were first sparked in many a young imagination: the beautiful "fear" of the majestic coasters, the "terror" of the dark rides, and the "adventure" of flight in the ROCKET SHIPS. No youngster was a mere audience to the spectacle; no youngster was a viewer of a two dimensional motion picture, but an active participant of a "grand" event.

There was a special world, a little world for the little folks. It was a place where those first fantasies of wooden horses, towering Ferris Wheels and miniature boats began. Each ride represented whatever creative experience the young passenger imagined; it could be different every time.

At Euclid Beach, the unique "little park" called KIDDIELAND was housed in the COLONNADE, a large concrete pavilion that also had inside picnic tables and refreshment stands. The giggles and screams echoed amid the sounds of dwarf-like rides while proud parents looked on with a FROZEN WHIP in hand.

(Illus. 126) "Whoa, Horsie! Yer goin' too fast," or at least so it seemed to the youngster at the time. This ride was a Euclid Beach original and was designed by Howard Stoneback.

(Illus. 127) Little engineers could run their own railroad even if it meant supplying their own power. The CHIEF proudly flew two flags. (Note the length of the woman's skirt.) (c. 1950)

(Randall Tiedman)

(Illus. 128) Amusement rides often reflect technical achievements of the day. The earlie KIDDIE CARS to appear at the park were located along the walkway from the streetc stop near the site of the COLONNADE.

(Kekic Collection)

(Illus. 129) "Hold on!" These young riders prepare to test the KIDDIE WHIP. This ride was a smaller version of W. F. Mangel's full sized "adult" WHIP. The painted flowery decor seems incongruous with the ride's mechanism.

(Illus. 130) The junior version of OVER-THE-FALLS was, as was its larger cousin, a Euclid Beach original. It, too, bore the Howard Stoneback signature. The course included a small hill and a mini plunge as a finale.

(Patty Souvain/Randall Tiedman)

(Richman Bros.)

(Illus. 131) Little ladies and gentlemen drivers off on a trip to anywhere they wish to go. Note the attire. Even the ride operator wears a coat and tie. (c. 1940)

(Illus. 132) Off to SLEEPY HOLLOW. T
locomotive was converted from its ori
nal steam power to that of compress
air. A refill was required after each tr
The conversion to compressed air w
done in the park's own shop.

(Richman Bros.)

(Illus. 133) A rock garden with little cascades of water
intrigued many of the youngsters who visited KIDDIE-
LAND.

(Illus. 134) The final miniature train to run the SLEEPY HOLLOW line was the EUCLID BEACH CHIEF, a diesel replica. The excursion lost little of its charm in later days. The track wove in and out of the RACING COASTER'S structure.

(Illus. 135) Two views of SLEEPY HOLLOW VILLAGE in the late Thirties. RACING COASTER trackage can be seen in the background.

WORKING AT PLAY

The unique character of Euclid Beach showed itself in many ways, but one of the most significant attributes of the park was the family closeness of the employees. This feature existed from the Humphrey acquisition of the Beach in 1901 until the last day, September 28, 1969. (Many members of the Euclid Beach family still work together at Shady Lake in Streetsboro, Ohio, a small park operated by the Humphrey Company, [1979]).

Those who worked at the Beach through its golden era are perhaps the most understanding of the Park's greatness and possess the most intimate affection for its memory. It was this family, under the direction of the Humphrey family, that spent the warm summers *and* the cold winters — WORKING AT PLAY.

(Illus. 136) This large house was one of the Humphrey residences. Located at the northeast corner of the property overlooking Lake Erie, this grand house was a year round home for the Humphreys.

(Robert Callaghan Collection)

(Illus. 137) Members of the Fay, Foote and Humphrey families gathered at a Fay Family reunion in 1900. They are: 1. Grandpa Jerimia Fay, 2. Grandma Mary Fay, 3. David Humphrey, 4. Louise Humphrey, 5. Will Fay, 6. D. S. Humphrey II, 7. "Linnie" Humphrey, 8. Jenny Fay, 9. Alfred Fay, 10. Harlow Humphrey, 11. Clarence Fay, 12. Eunice Fay Foote, 13. Lloyd Foote.

(Eunice Foote)

(Illus. 140)

(Illus. 139)

(Illus. 138)

(Illus. 141)

(Illus. 144)

(Illus. 143)

(Illus. 142)

93

"Tickets—Not Money"

The universal ticket system is carried on to the last letter in Euclid Beach

THERE are certain shrewd subleties about the management and the policies of Euclid Beach Park which present themselves to your attention only after you have attentively studied this fine resort.

Perhaps the quickest way to discover these subleties is by comparison with other parks. The Humphrey management has shaped Euclid Beach Park to fit exactly the tastes and desires of the largest number of patrons that could be expected to come to it.

Therefore Euclid Beach Park, although it is a big park and a clean one and a refined one, has no "high hat" atmosphere—and no "low hat" attraction either. The Humphrey management has accomplished the happy medium. It is not managed to attract particularly the higher class of patron that is seen at Rye's Playland, for instance, nor the numerous type that masses in Coney Island, New York. It is managed to attract everybody and to make them feel at home.

Not too many decorations, not too much landscaping, no buildings that look as if it might cost a lot of money to go into them—just plain but substantial and satisfying amusement fare that gives dime for dime value. It might not go in some locations but there is no doubt about it being a success at Euclid Beach.

Money Submerged

"Perhaps," Mr. Humphrey remarked to the writer, "we don't know how to run a park —but here it is."

The subject of money is kept submerged as much as possible at this park. Nowhere, from the beginning to the end of a visit there, is it compulsory to spend money. No one asks you to, no one yells at you, no one urges you to spend a dime. In fact, it is possible to spend an entire and happy day at the park without giving up one cent.

"Tickets—Not Money"

"Tickets—Not Money." That is one of the slogans of the park. Every cent that comes from a patron, with the exception of the cafeteria and two small stands, goes into the universal ticket booths. There the patron receives strips of tickets good for five cents each—as many or as few as he wishes to buy.

It is easier to comprehend the extent to which this "Tickets—Not Money" slogan has been carried in Euclid Beach Park when you realize that even refreshment and soft drink stands accept tickets only. Loganberry, two tickets, ginger ale, one ticket, etc.

There are no barkers. No spielers invite you to step in or take a ride. No frankfurter

man informs you that they are "red hot." It isn't necessary, somehow, in Euclid Beach. You sense that everything is as it should be before you've been in the park five minutes.

The people of Cleveland trust the Humphreys and they trust Euclid Beach Park They are a Cleveland institution. There seems to be no doubt in anybody's mind—whether or not he is a patron—that what the Humphreys say or do is all right. No one thinks of mistrusting a ride or a refreshment.

Let us take the loganberry juice stand, for instance. A sign above the counter tells us that this juice is shipped directly to the park from the west coast, the home of loganberries. And you can believe this writer when he says that this loganberry drink at Euclid Beach is one of the best, if not the best, drink sold in any amusement park.

Even the creamy whip at Euclid Beach is something more than sweetened bubbles—it is as satisfying as a dish of ice cream. And the candy—that is made right before your eyes with real butter, and real cream and sugar. It's no wonder the people of Cleveland trust the Humphreys.

Know Him Personally

And a good many of them know Dudley S. Humphrey personally. They know him by sight, and they do not hesitate to speak to him whenever they see him. And the children— most all of them can recognize that electric wheel chair of his a mile off—flock around him. It's "Hello, Mister Humphrey" and Mr. Humphrey this and Mr. Humphrey that.

"They're alright," he remarked reflectively with a glint of amusement in his eyes one day, "but they're all little politicians, those kids."

Sure they are. But many of those kids have thought of him and his park during the winter months and during the long, tedious school hours—and that's success for an amusement park if anything is.

(The Humphrey Company)

(Illus. 138) Ben Seaman, Sr., was the Kiddieland manager. The date is 1944.

(M. Gandee Collection)

(Illus. 139) Howard Stoneback came to the Beach with the Philadelphia Toboggan Company for the construction of the THRILLER in 1924. He became the head of engineering and stayed at the park until his death in 1958. Mr. Stoneback was responsible for many ride designs and park innovations.

(William Stoneback Collection)

(Illus. 140) Dudley Sherman Humphrey II was the guiding force behind Euclid Beach Park from its 1901 purchase until his death in 1933. Here he is seated in a three wheeled car especially designed for him by the Custer Co. of Dayton. This firm constructed a number of rides for the park. The date is September, 1932.

(The Humphrey Company)

(Illus. 141) Don Ressler at the controls of the SLEEPY HOLLOW locomotive. Compressed air is being fed into the train's tender.

(Donald Ressler Collection)

(Illus. 142) Mike Mower, SLEEPY HOLLOW RAILROAD engineer, loads the tender with compressed air. This process was repeated after each trip.

(Donald Ressler Collection)

(Illus. 143) Bill Conway and a young companion. Mr. Conway was the park's electrician.

(William Stoneback Collection)

(Illus. 144) Perc Killally, Purchasing Director, became part of the Humphrey family, and in turn part of the Euclid Beach family.

(The Humphrey Company)

(Illus. 146) Three views of the park shop. These scenes show where many original ideas came to life to provide patrons of the park with rides and improvements that became identified with Euclid Beach.

(William Stoneback Collection)

(Illus. 147) Harvey Humphrey marked the second generation of Humphreys to operate Euclid Beach Park. Here he is pictured (top left) with his wife and Mr. and Mrs. Howard Stoneback.

(William Stoneback Collection)

(Illus. 148) Winter has set in as snow covers the cottages that housed many of the park employees. While it seems to be a sleepy scene the park's shop was probably humming with preparation for the next season.

(William Stoneback Collection)

(Illus. 149) This April, 1930 photograph reveals the construction of the FLYING TURNS in progress. The workman levels the footers for that section of the ride leading to the chain-lift. In the background is the building that houses the WITCHING WAVES ride. This structure, later enclosed, housed the LAFF-IN-THE-DARK. Just in front is part of the ZOOMER, a Custer Co. ride that appeared at the Beach for a short time.

(Robert Callaghan Collection)

(Illus. 150) Art Steele was a Euclid Beach perennial and is here pictured by the paddle wheel of the OVER-THE-FALLS.

(Illus. 151) Here Art Steele (third from right) is posed with his high-ride crew (THRILLER, RACING COASTER and FLYING TURNS) on the THRILLER unloading platform. The date—September 28, 1969, the last day.

(Arthur Steele Collection)

96

BEAUTY AND THE BEACH

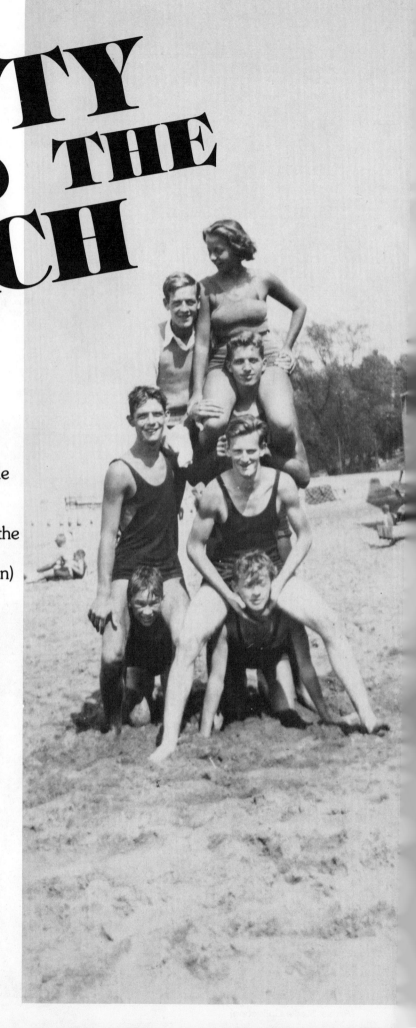

From the time when a peek at a woman's ankle was daring and bathing suits were made of wool . . . until "progress" denied us Lake Erie as a place to swim . . . from an era of strolling on the sand with a parasol . . . until the algae drove us from the beaches . . . that narrow strip of golden sand (it really was clean) attracted millions to Euclid Beach Park.

Lovely young ladies in the latest bathing attire, lapping waves and summer sunshine brought together "beauty and the BEACH."

(Illus. 152) Five scenes showing bathers and lifeguards on the BEACH and in the circular pool in the early 1930s. Among them are members of the Seaman and Crosby families (the Crosbys of Crosby-On-the-Lake restaurant that was located on the second floor of the BATHHOUSE.

(M. Gandee Collection)

(Illus. 154) "Sailing, sailing, over the bounding" BEACH. A young visitor sits in one of the boats from the LIVERY available for rental.

(Illus. 155) Lovely cargo is stowed in this vessel. The waves are seen breaking behind these two young ladies and the PIER seems busy with visitors.

(Parmadale Collection)

(Illus. 153) The PIER, the FOUNTAIN and the BATHHOUSE, how familiar they seem. Some people stroll while fishermen patiently await a strike as they occupy lower levels on each side of the PIER.

(Richman Bros.)

(Illus. 157) Facing top—Truly beauty and the beach. A beauty contest proceeds on a promenade constructed on the BEACH. There are straw hats a-plenty and the band waits to salute the winner. The FOUNTAIN and the BATHHOUSE can be seen in the background.

(Robert Callaghan Collection)

(Illus. 158) Facing bottom—Beauty everywhere! Bathing beauties compete as part of a Richman Brothers annual picnic. They are pictured in front of the stage in the DANCE PAVILION.

(Richman Bros.)

(Illus. 156) A lifeguard, in the bathing suit style of the day, stands in front of the BATHHOUSE.

(M. Gandee Collection)

(Illus. 159) Top—There were many ways to camp at the park. Here vintage cars with tents stand in front of the TOURIST KITCHEN. The building now houses the trailer park office.

(Illus. 160) Bottom—The AUTO TRAIN moves through the CAMP-GROUNDS fully loaded with passengers. This tour was a slow, peaceful ride around much of the grounds. The amusement and camping area were both on the route. Many might debate the appeal of such a ride today. (1979)

(Illus. 161) Facing top—Many families spent all or part of thei summers at a rented cabin at the CAMPGROUNDS of Euclid Beach These cabins were built of poured cement based on the Humphre Company's own process. A trailer park now occupies this site.

(Illus. 162) Facing middle—A group of small cabins that were availabl for summer rental. The CAMPGROUNDS were just east of the mai amusement area. Many remember soft summer nights amid the Syca more trees and falling to sleep to the sounds of the THRILLER, bar organ music and the distant laughs and screams of the many visito to the Beach.

(Illus. 163) Facing bottom—The beauty of the setting can be seen this view of the cabins and CAMPGROUNDS.

(Robert Callaghan Collection)

(Robert Callaghan Collection)

(William Stoneback Collection)

104

SOME

(Illus. 164) With plenty of shade, picnicking was popular in the early days of Euclid Beach's history. This area was near the GROVE LUNCH which later became the site of the COLONNADE.

(Russell Allon Hehr Collection

CAME TO EAT

There were those who could not resist a ride on the THRILLER or a whirl on the CARROUSEL. Some of the visitors were lured by the BEACH and the cooling lake. Others twirled about on the infinite dance floor or roller skated to the grand GAVIOLI. There were those who wished to just sit and observe, or there were patrons who played MINIATURE GOLF, SKEE BALL or the games in the PENNY ARCADE.

Apart from these was a dedicated group with one thing on its mind . . . the "tasty" delights at the BEACH. Yes, there were the avid riders, players, swimmers, dancers and skaters, but . . . Some Came to Eat!

(Illus. 165) The FROZEN WHIP was irresistible, a hall-mark of the Beach, and was not just a frozen custard. It was also messy.

(Russell Allon Hehr Collection)

(Illus. 166) The hot dog was a basic constituent of a Euclid Beach visitor's appetite. The "dogs" were being dispensed at the lunch stand in the COLONNADE.

(The Humphrey Company)

(Illus. 167) Humphrey POP CORN was a unique product made of specially grown Japanese hull-less kernels. People of all ages enjoyed this Euclid Beach treat.

(The Humphrey Company)

108

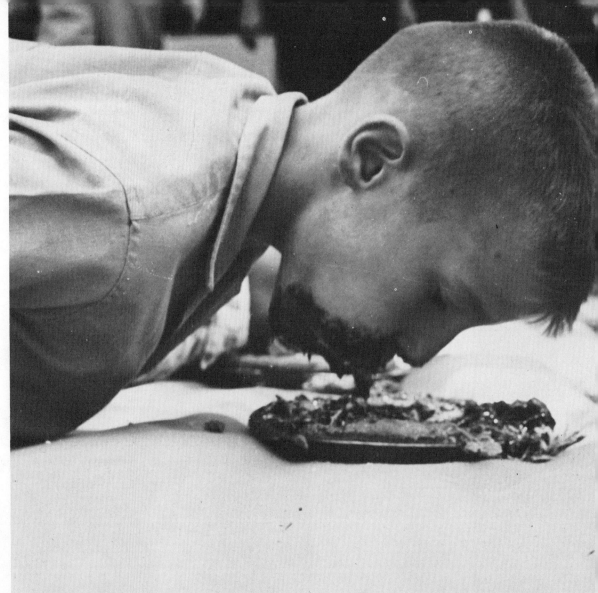

(Illus. 168) "Ready, aim, eat!" These young boys were engaged in a messy business—a pie eating contest at one of the Richman Brothers picnics.

(Richman Bros.)

(Richman Bros.)

(Illus. 169) With a POPCORN BALL eater on each knee, this Richman Brothers executive is host to two young Euclid Beach enthusiasts.

(Parmadale Collection)

(Illus. 170) The enjoyment of the moment is apparent by the "look" on this boy's face. A real "two-fisted" FROZEN WHIP eater.

THEY GATHERED TOGETHER

Every summer brought a day, a very special day, looked forward to by young and old alike. This was the day of the annual picnic or outing and it was anticipated with a fervor akin to that of the arrival of Santa Claus. For some it was sponsored by an employer, for others by a community or lodge. The American Automobile Association brought the orphans to the Beach, and record crowds with attendant traffic jams came from Akron and the rubber companies.

They gathered together to ride, to play, to talk, to generally socialize with people with whom they worked or served; they came to celebrate summer, fellowship, recreation and life. Perhaps, without so proclaiming, they also celebrated Euclid Beach Park.

(Illus. 171) The magnitude of some of the annual picni proclaimed by the front page announcement. The major rubber manufacturing companies in Akron, Go rich and Goodyear, brought some of the largest cro to the park.

(The Humphrey Company)

The Akron Times-Press

WEATHER—Fair today; fair and warmer tomorrow.

PICNIC SPECIAL

PRICE THREE CENTS

No. 10,630   IN TWO SECTIONS — SECTION ONE   AKRON, OHIO, MONDAY, AUGUST 8, 1932   Entered as second class matter, Post Office, Akron, Ohio.

GOODRICH IS HOST TO 40,000
Seiberling Workers Hold Annual Frolic

WORK IS FORGOTTEN AT 'PLAY DAY' EVENT

Miniature Beauty Queen Chosen as Hundreds Compete in Contests

By TED COX
Times-Press Staff Writer

CLEVELAND, Aug. 8.—Nearly 40,000 Goodrich rubber workers and their families were at Euclid beach here today for the annual "play day" of the company.

The big parade of workers started before 6 o'clock this morning. And with a long train, 47 buses and more than 20,000 automobiles, the parade continued throughout the morning, diminishing the population of Akron by almost one-sixth.

The entire Goodrich plant at Akron was closed as all employes forgot worries and work to join in the world's largest industrial picnic. All Goodrich people, with the exception of directors who were in New York for a meeting, were present.

The big event of the day came when the time-honored bathing beauty contest was turned over to the children. Joane Dickinson, 3-year-old daughter of Mr. and Mrs. H. T. Dickinson, 1179 Mount Vernon street, was judged the prettiest girl over nearly 40 competitors.

The most handsome boy honors went to Charles Skidmore, 4-year-old son of E. C. Skidmore, 667 Clearview road.

Introduce Veterans

Following the contest the oldest employes in the company's personnel were introduced from the speaker's platform.

Hundreds of persons took part in the elaborate program of athletic contests. More than $800 in prize money was to make the "play day" a profitable one for several winners.

First information concerning Akron Day at the National Air races was brought to the thousands assembled at the park thru a public address system. Clifford W. Henderson, manager of the races, and E. W. "Pop" Cleveland, chairman of the contest committee, outlined the attractions.

Everybody Happy

All concessions in the park were crowded with both children and grown-ups trying to cram in all the features in the limited time of one day.

Thousands of children were plunging into the waters of Lake Erie for free bathing.

Old-time dancing was offered during the day. The program will be completed with the grand ball tonight in the Euclid Beach dance hall.

Fifty girls, each representing a division, dressed as stunningly as possible, were to parade before the judges as one of the climatic features. The winner was to receive her award from Mrs. T. G. Graham, wife of T. G. Graham, Goodrich vice-president.

Members of the play-day committee, wearing shining helmets to identify them, kept things going. The committee concluded: A. C. Sprague, C. T. Butler, J. E. Gulick, F. A. Lang, H. J. Zimmerman, E. Straiton, B. A. Evans, J. V. James, W. L. Herbruck, R. Johnston, J. F. Haemmerlin, Dr. L. E. Lowe, E. K. Davis and R. F. Snyder.

PARK IS THRONGED BY MERRY MAKERS

Hundreds at Summit Beach For Games and Annual Picnic Dinner

Gay, carefree throngs, swelled the casual park-visiting around at Summit Beach park late this afternoon as hundreds of Seiberling Rubber company employes and their families met for their annual picnic.

Parking grounds were congested as car after car of picnickers arrived. Little family groups—supper baskets in hand. They met at the north end tables to check their baskets and then drifted thru the park playgrounds, not to meet again until eating activities brought them back.

The swimming pool was crowded with children who splashed in safety at the lower end of the pool while older people claimed diving boards at the other end. Concessions, ice cream, cone

stands and iced drink counters were busy.

By 3 p. m. the crowd gathered at the athletic field for games and contests. There were events for all members of the family.

Starters for the events were Paul Mandru and Ray Demas. Prizes were presented by C. W. Seiberling. Dancing was in order thruout the afternoon and will continue this evening.

The committee in charge included R. E. Vanatta, A. S. Bechtel, William Evans, C. W. Cockrell, E. R. Neyland, D. R. Bunnard, Art Johnson, George Jones, E. R. Gibson, H. A. Walters, W. Andrews and Seiberling.

Employes of the Seiberling Latex Products company and the Kemiles company participated in the general outing.

WHITE MOTOR IS BUSY

CLEVELAND, Aug. 8.—White Motor company today was starting work on a $1,000,000 order for trucks from the United States government. The order was received late in June. It calls for 485 units for the postal service. No additional men will be added at this time.

Here are scenes from the Goodrich and Seiberling picnics which drew tens of thousands to playgrounds. The white circles around their heads have a special significance all their own. Those people whose heads are circled can get a pair of tickets to the RKO Palace theater, good this week, free of charge by bringing a paper to The Times-Press and identifying themselves. The scenes pictured above at the Goodrich picnic are, No. 1—Hundreds of parents gathered for the beauty contest. No. 2—Joane Dickinson, 3, and Charles Skidmore, 4, beauty contest winners. No. 3—Shoe race. No. 4—Women's 50-yard dash. No. 5—Baby parade. No. 6—The Goodrich committee, front row, A. Felton, J. A. Devereux, N. Pappano, J. F. Haemmerlin, David Straiton; back row G. Shriber, E. Davis, C. F. Butler, A. C. Sprague and R. Straiton. No. 7—Hundreds crowded the free rides. No. 8—Seiberling picnickers. No. 9—Boys' Sack race.

PICKS 9700 POTATO BUGS

By United Press
GREENSBURG, Pa., Aug. 8.—A total of 9700 potato bugs were picked from an acre of potatoes in little more than a month by James Black, Salem township farmer. Black is sure of the count. For each bug he placed a small stone in a basket he carried with him. After completing his rounds, he counted the pebbles.

Tickets Offered In Picnic Photos

Watch for The Akron Times-Press Picnic Pictures—and see if you're in nothing.

Starting today, heads of picnickers photographed by The Times-Press cameramen at various outings, will be circled when published in the paper.

Anyone who comes to The Times-Press office with a paper and identifies him or herself as the person whose head is circled will get a pair of tickets to R-K-O Palace free.

Goodrich and Seiberling workers should watch late editions of today's Times-Press for free tickets.

There are three lucky circles on Page 9 in this edition.

CANOPY FALLS; TWO DEAD

By United Press
NEW ORLEANS, La., Aug. 8.—A 26-ton steel and concrete building canopy which fell onto a sidewalk here killed two persons and injured four others, a police check showed today.

The dead were Thomas Moore, 60, shipping clerk, and William Quaid, 45, clerk.

KILLED HUGE DOGFISH

By United Press
REVERE, Mass. Aug 8.—Lawson Smith Jr. killed a 40-pound dogfish after a struggle when it attacked and bit him while he was swimming off Oak Island, near here, recently.

114

(Illus. 172) The Sisters from Parmadale brought orphans in their charge to Euclid Beach. These were very special days for everybody concerned, and MANY people were CONCERNED. For the employees of the Park this was a cherished opportunity to serve. The year is 1938, with tie, straw hat and vintage buses.

(Illus. 174) (Facing) The Parmadale Band is ready for the downbeat as they wait in front of the MAIN GATE. (1938)

(Illus. 173) The Cleveland Automobile Club was a sponsor of the Orphan's Days from early in the century beginning with 1903.

63rd Outing

AS ALWAYS, a great time was had by all! The Club's 63rd Annual Outing July 6-7 thrilled 359 boys and girls (shut-ins, infants and the hospitalized) at eight institutions and 2,464 others from 18 homes, agencies and foster homes, at Euclid Beach.

A 50-member committee of officials and civic leaders did the honors, both for the first day's institutional visits and for the next day at Euclid Beach, helping serve the box lunch at noon.

For many years, until 1959, ⊕ Members had the option of contributing to the Outing Fund at the time of dues payments. The Fund now is self-sustaining, from interest.

CLEVELAND AAA OHIO AUTOMOBILE CLUB

1966

PUTTING lesson, at Euclid Beach miniature golf course, by nun from Parmadale.

EUCLID BEACH Outing participants ranged from babes in arms to rambunctious teen-agers, from 18 institutions and hundreds of foster. This young lady grins for the camera while aboard a galloping merry-go-round steed.

DISTRIBUTING caps, gum, balloons and novelties at amusement park entrance were Club Board Chairman John F. Patt, Dudley Humphrey, Jr. of the amusement park Humphreys, and Beach Manager E.P. Shilliday.

AL ROSEN, former Indians third base great, now a stock broker, with friends at Rose-Mary Home. Al's new on the Committee.

115

(Parmadale Collection)

(Illus. 175) Old Classmates Day at Euclid Beach, 1933. The Beach was a natural place for such an event.

(Illus. 176) The LOG CABIN served as a picnic headquarters throughout its history at the park.

(Illus. 177) They're off and running! These eager picnickers compete in one of the field events held on the athletic field near the coasters. The RACING COASTER is at the left, then the top of the THRILLER'S first hill is visible and part of the FLYING TURNS barrel and support structure is on the right. (1933)

(Russell Allon Hehr Collection)

(Illus. 178) Picnickers from the Loyal Order of Moose pose in cars of the AERO DIPS. The braking mechanism located between the rails is angular rather than the later flat friction brake used on the THRILLER and RACING COAST-ER. The AERO DIPS was a 1909 John A. Miller coaster of moderate size but with maximal enjoyment. This picture is dated August 25, 1932.

(Russell Allon Hehr Collection

118

THE EAST CLEVELAND SIGNAL
The Signal Is the Official Newspaper for the City of East Cleveland

FIRST COMMUNITY PICNIC JULY 22

BIG DAY FOR KIDDIES WITH ALL KINDS OF PRIZES AND CONTESTS

Merchants Give Merchandise and Purchase Cash Prize Tickets Liberally; List of Donors Will Be Published Next Week

ANOTHER PLAY BY KIWANIANS

You'll See Them At The Picnic

THE EAST CLEVELAND SIGNAL
The Signal Is the Official Newspaper for the City of East Cleveland

ONLY NEWSPAPER IN EAST CLEVELAND
Only $1.00 Per Year

STAGE SET FOR COMMUNITY PICNIC JULY
City Plans Community Band Concert At Stadium

His Band Plays For Picnic Dance

Plan 37th
Community P
At Euclid Be

More Than $1,000 in Prizes Listed on Inside Pages

EAST CLEVELAND
Community Picnic News
Published for the Community Picnic Committee by the East Cleveland Signal

Prepare for Record Crowd at Sixth Annual Picnic July 15

EUCLID BEACH PARK FROM THE AIR

Expect 40,000 for Outing at Euclid Beach

$200 Electric Refrigerator Heads Picnic Prize List

More Than 500 Gifts Offered by Merchants

Ticket Demand Largest Ever Experienced

CITY TO CLOSE SHOPS HALF DAY FOR OUTING

Log Cabin Again Will Be Used as Headquarters

Girls set for 40 yard dash.

Three leggers, William Abbott and Richard Lampe.

Mayor Kenneth Sims presents prize to Josephine Lukushka.

Sally Henderson and James Waters.

Twins Beverly and Sally

The East Cleveland Signal
EAST CLEVELAND'S ONLY NEWSPAPER ...SINCE 1900

ONLY NEWSPAPER OF EAST CLEVELAND, COLONIAL HEIGHTS AND NOBLE ROAD AREA

10,000 Guaranteed Circulation Every Thursday

EXPECT 40,000 AT ANNUAL PICNIC

Committees Responsible for Success of Community Picnic

Record-Breaking Crowd E

RECORD CROWD TO ATTEND CITY'S 10th OUTING AT EUCLID BEACH WEDNESDA

Merchants Offer Hundreds of Prizes; Picnic To Have Full Day of Sports, Games, Ride And Amusements at Park

HARRY F. MARTIN

FRED A HENDERSON

L. W. LAUBE

DR. J. A. STAHL

KARL BROWN

G. O. P. Plans

Transportation Schedule

Chief Asks

THE EAST CLEVELAND SIGNAL
The Signal Is the Official Newspaper for the City of East Cleveland

PICNIC VERY GRATIFYING SUCCE

"Patrolman Burns' Corner Closed"

GOES TO RUSSIA FOR M'KEE CO.

REGISTRATION TICKET SUP EXHAUSTED EARLY IN AFTE

CUT OUT NOISE

20,000 EAST CLEVELANDERS PICNIC

(The Humphrey Company)

(Illus. 180) East Cleveland was a community that always sponsored a large and enthusiastically attended "event."

(Illus. 181)   (Richman Bros.)

(Illus. 182)

121

(Illus. 181, 182, 183, 184) The LOG CABIN functioned as headquarters for the Richman Brothers picnic. It was here that guests registered, received their ride and refreshment tickets and entered the various drawings and contests. Richman Brothers was one of a number of nationally prominent companies to treat their families of workers to a special day at Euclid Beach Park.

(Richman Bros.)   (Illus. 183)

(Illus. 184)

(Illus. 185)

(Illus. 185, 186) As a special day for the ladies each woman had the opportunity to radiate her beauty and/or make a fool herself. All this was in the name of fun.

(Richman Bros.) (Illus. 186)

(Illus. 187, 188, 189, 190, 191, 1
Everyone joined in the games fr
the highest executive to the you
est toddler. Picnic sports rang
from softball to the egg toss.

(Richman Bros.)

(Illus. 189)

(Illus. 191)

(Illus. 192)

(Illus. 190)

126

Be our guest
on
16 FREE RIDES
including
THE THRILLER
at
EUCLID BEACH PARK

WEDNESDAY, JUNE 28
4:00 P. M. to 11:30 P. M.

GET BADGES HERE
Headquarters at the MAIN DANCE HALL
PROGRAM

(Illus. 193)

TWENTY-NINTH ANNUAL
EAST CLEVELAND
COMMUNITY PICNIC
EUCLID BEACH PARK
WEDNESDAY, JULY 15, 1959

GRAND PRIZE

1959 CHEVROLET
BISCAYNE 2-DOOR SEDAN
(Winner Pays All State and Federal Taxes)
(MUST WINNER MUST BE 18 YEARS OF AGE OR OVER)

You Must Be Present With Ticket Stub To Win Automobile or Major Prizes

Car Through Co-operation of Jim Cassell Chevrolet, Inc., 14481 Euclid Avenue

DRAWING ON AUTO — 9:00 P. M. SHARP

Merchant's Exposition In Log Cabin

Public AUTO SHOW FEATURING NEW 1959 MODELS

SEE THE EXCITING STYLES AND COLORS ON DISPLAY

Do Not Fail To Ask For Picnic Tickets From Your Merchants Of East Cleveland
Sponsored by East Cleveland Merchants in Appreciation of Patronage by Our Customers

BOYS' AND GIRLS' SPORT EVENTS START AT 2 P. M.

OVER $5,000.00 IN FREE PRIZES

Better Appliances For Better Homes   RCA Whirlpool

GIRLS' ZLES

RCA MODEL X 80 WHIRLPOOL SWEEPER $89.95 VALUE

RCA MODEL G 313 GAS RANGE $279.95 VALUE

RCA MODEL ED 25 GAS DRYER $219.95 VALUE

EAST CLEVELAND COMMUNITY PICNIC COMMITTEE

(Illus. 194)

35th Annual East Cleveland
COMMUNITY PICNIC
WEDNESDAY, JULY 21, 1965
EUCLID BEACH PARK

First Prize . . . $300.00
Second Prize . . . $100.00
4 Portable T.V's
4 Transistor Radios

FREE AND REDUCED RIDES

Games and Contests for the Kids
FUN FOR THE WHOLE FAMILY

(Illus. 195)

(Illus. 193, 194, 195, 196) Examples of promotional posters for East Cleveland Community Picnics.

(Harry "Pepper" Martin)

PICNIC OFFICIALS FROLIC. Staid East Cleveland Community chairmen and other officials will cover Euclid Beach next Wednesday like a blanket to see that the 32nd annual event is the best ever. This artist's conception of what they will be doing was drawn for the East Cleveland Leader by a young art student, George Vidmar, who is destined to go places. Starting at the left ... a putt in typical picnic style is Charles MacDonald. Coming through the entrance in an unusual fashion are front Dick Pearce, Ray Snydam and Lou Planic; up in about the whole thing in their rocket ship are Fred Henderson, Cuttler and Wilson Rich; coming down the roller coaster typical committee fashion are front to back Margaret We...

(Illus. 196)

You Are Invited To Attend
THE EAST CLEVELAND COMMUNITY PICNIC

All Day Wednesday, July 22nd. — 1931

STARTING AT 9:00 A. M.

AT EUCLID BEACH PARK

Put everything else aside and attend this Community Day, the first of its kind in East Cleveland. Make it a gala gathering of East Cleveland people. The merchants of all East Cleveland have worked and planned for months to make this a great day for their friends and customers. Show them your appreciation for their efforts by attending 40,000 strong.

$ CASH PRIZES—YES 49 OF THEM $

From $5.00 to $25.00, in Real Money! Ask Any East Cleveland Merchant for Tickets—They Are FREE! Deposit Stubs at Park.

IMPORTANT!—Registration prizes to the extent of 400 or more items of merchandise (a complete list appears on another page of this program). Tickets for these prizes may be purchased for 10c each in front of the Log Cabin at Euclid Beach. Each ticket you purchase has attached to it Five Free Five-Cent Tickets good for rides for children 14 years and under. You may buy as many tickets as you like as long as the limited supply lasts. For each 10c you get 25c worth of tickets and a chance on the list of prizes, which in an aggregate sum are worth $2,000 or more.

Some of the registration tickets will be put on advance sale at a few East Cleveland stores, as listed below.

GENERAL ANNOUNCEMENT

Be sure to register. Each registration entitles you to a chance on more than 400 prizes. Registration tables are in front of the Log Cabin.

When you register you can get a strip of tickets for the kiddies. The supply is limited, so register early and get yours. Each ticket is good for five cents if used for a ride, or at the theater.

The drawings for the registration prizes and cash prizes will be held about 4:00 p. m. and in the order named, on the band stand on the west side of the Log Cabin. The drawing for dance prizes will be held at 11:00 p. m. at the Log Cabin.

There will be dancing at the Log Cabin from 2:30 to 5:30 and from 7:00 until closing. Each strip of dance tickets entitles you and your partner to two double dances and a chance on 100 prizes. A strip of tickets costs 10 cents.

If you win first, second or third place in any of the games you will immediately receive a ticket which entitles you to a prize and will tell you where to secure it, if your number wins in any of the drawings, go to George N. Nelson, Jeweler and Optician, 1385 Hayden ave., and present your stub with the winning number and you will receive an order for the prize.

PHIL G. WUERTZ HARDWARE
1395 Hayden Avenue

GEORGE N. NELSON, JEWELER
1385 Hayden Avenue

McGRATH HARDWARE CO.
13587 Euclid Avenue

HOFFMAN-CARLSON—PRINTERS
14066 Euclid Avenue

HUMMEL-DETERING CO.
1620 Hayden Avenue

MODEL VARIETY STORE
1410 Hayden Avenue

EUCLID-TAYLOR PHARMACY
15470 Euclid Avenue

MED-ART DRESS SHOPPE
16351 Euclid Avenue

ATHLETIC EVENTS START AT 10:30 A. M. SHARP. EAST CLEVELAND STORES WILL BE CLOSED ALL DAY WEDNESDAY, JULY 22, BUT WILL BE OPEN UNTIL 9:00 P. M. TUESDAY EVENING.

All money received from ticket sales is used to pay the cost of this picnic.

All prizes must be called for at Nelson Jewelry Store, 1385 Hayden Ave., before Wednesday, July 29. Be sure to bring your winning stub with you. Winning numbers will be published in The East Cleveland Signal and will be posted on store windows in East Cleveland.

FAC SIMILE OF REGISTRATION TICKET

No. 1000
E. C. Community Day
REGISTRATION
1931
SAVE THIS FOR PRIZE

Name
Address
DROP THIS STUB IN BOX
REGISTRATION
1931

No. 1000
E. C. Community Day

CHILDREN'S TICKET
14 Years or Under
Good for 5c Towards
ONE RIDE
E. C. COMMUNITY DAY
JULY 22, 1931
EUCLID BEACH PARK

CHILDREN'S TICKET
14 Years or Under
Good for 5c Towards
ONE RIDE
E. C. COMMUNITY DAY
JULY 22, 1931
EUCLID BEACH PARK

CHILDREN'S TICKET
14 Years or Under
Good for 5c Towards
ONE RIDE
E. C. COMMUNITY DAY
JULY 22, 1931
EUCLID BEACH PARK

CHILDREN'S TICKET
14 Years or Under
Good for 5c Towards
ONE RIDE
E. C. COMMUNITY DAY
JULY 22, 1931
EUCLID BEACH PARK

CHILDREN'S TICKET
14 Years or Under
Good for 5c Towards
ONE RIDE
E. C. COMMUNITY DAY
JULY 22, 1931
EUCLID BEACH PARK

(Harry "Pepper" Martin)   (Illus. 198)

(Illus. 199) "Dig into the barrel and pull out a winner." This was a familiar scene at many annuals. Drawings were held on the OUTDOOR STAGE near the LOG CABIN. Here a winner collects her prize during the 1964 Addressograph-Multigraph outing.

(Tom Satyrshur Collection)

It's a time for ruffled pink dresses on prim little girls . . .

(Illus. 200) Some fitting remarks about a day at the Beach

(Tom Satyrshur Collection)

The Company Picnic is a special event for AM employees.

It's a time for ruffled pink dresses on prim little girls and newly starched shirts on squirming little boys. It's a time for cotton candy and popcorn and hamburgers and hot dogs with slaps of mustard. It's quite a day for the entire family, as the pictures in this month's AM NEWS prove. Too soon, it seemed, the picnic was over and the world of cotton candy quietly melted.

The 17 field events left a deep impression of what it takes to be a winner —you have to be the best in the competition to win. The fastest runners won the races . . . the most accurate marksmen hit the targets . . . the most careful tosses won the egg-throwing contests.

(Illus. 201) A-M News, company house organ cover, 1967 issue.

(Tom Satyrshur Collection)

(Illus. 202, 203) Political rallies frequented the Beach. In 1965 a Democratic Party function featured such nationally known figures as Teddy Kennedy and local dignitaries.

(Michael A. Fuerst Collection)

(Illus. 203)

133

(Michael A. Fuerst Collection)

(Illus. 204)

134

Not all the visitors who traveled in circles at Euclid Beach were on the CARROUSEL or riding the ROCKET SHIPS. Dancers whirled across a spacious dance floor on a polished glaze. They seemed to float as if airborne, never touching the surface of gleaming wood. Dance bands with well remembered names provided romantic and lilting melodies for dancers, many of whom came to the Beach only to trip the light fantastic.

Nearby, bordered by the AERO DIPS (a moderate roller coaster), a lunch counter, the PENNY ARCADE, and the Humphrey estate, was another Euclid Beach favorite, the ROLLER RINK. From 1904 to 1962, the rink was a center for dedicated skaters who moved on wooden wheels to the sounds of the grand and glorious GAVIOLI band organ. This instrument is internationally known as one of the finest examples of the band organ.

Whether they were dancers or skaters there was the lilt of music and a feeling of romance as visitors to the Beach went round and round.

(Richman Bros.)

(Illus. 206) The DANCE PAVILION was one of the original structures erected at the park (designed by Knox and Elliot, prominent Cleveland architects). During its lifetime it underwent changes both internally and externally. This post card depicts the PAVILION in the early part of the century. The building met its end in 1972 at the hands of vandals who set fire to the wooden edifice.

(Russell Allon Hehr Collection)

ROUND and ROUND

(Illus. 207) John Currier was one of the earliest musicians to lead a band in Euclid Beach's BALLROOM. The ensemble is here pictured on the north balcony bandstand. The globe lights indicate the picture was taken early in the Twentieth century.

(Illus. 208) The "jitterbug" and "twist" pose a sharp contrast to the Currier days of the "moonlight waltz" and 1920's "two-step". The interior of the PAVILION shows the art-deco lights suspended from the ceiling in this 1950's picture.

(Richman Bros.)

(Illus. 209, 210) The DANCE PAVILION also served as picnic headquarters and beauty contest sight in the later years of the park's operation.

(Illus. 211)

(Richman Bros.)

(Illus. 210)

139

(Illus. 211, 212, 213) The ROLLER RINK featured a maple floor, the magnificent GAVIOLI band organ and sides that opened to let the soft summer air in and melodious rhythms out. Just as the DANCE PAVILION provided a meeting place for young men and women, the ROLLER RINK also set the stage for many a romance.

(Willis Zeitz Collection)

(Illus. 213)

(James Worgull Collection)
(Illus. 214)

(James Worgull Collection)
(Illus. 215)

(Illus. 214, 215) The GAVIOLI band organ that furnished the music for the ROLLER RINK during most of the rink's existence orginally was placed in the LYCEUM, Cleveland's first major indoor ice-skating rink. Unsuccessful in that function, the glorious machine found a home at Euclid Beach. These two views show the organ's grand facade and some of the pipes and mechanism at the rear.

DANCE PAVILION

(Illus. 216) Faded glory is reflected in the closed windows of the old PAVILION. The trees are bare, the bandstand silent, the floor empty: the "Beach is closed for the season".

IMPRESSIONS

Every generation of visitors to Euclid Beach retained varying sets of impressions of the park. To a good many it was the scene of a meeting with someone who became a life-long partner in marriage. To others the taste of a different kiss remains on the taste buds, and the crunch of the POPCORN BALLS and POPCORN and the ever messy FROZEN WHIP remains vivid. Some still smell the "hot grease" that swam up to the nostrils as the THRILLER clacked up the big hill. For others it was the echo of the "merry-go-round" sounds or those of a favorite dance band. Whether it be the annual picnic or a casual evening visit (something that is almost impossible to do at an amusement park today), the impression is indelible. And why should any of these impressions be deleted from the experiences of other times? Things of value never grow old, just distant.

Euclid Beach Park represented the attainment of an ideal to a greater degree than so many other of man's efforts, and through that attainment the impressions are as if sculpted on granite. They have constantly emerged throughout the years since the Beach's close: in verse; rhyme; photo; and painting — all recalling the impressions.

(Illus. 217) The "magic entrance" at night. The structure still stands as a Cleveland landmark.

(Harry Luikart Collection)

CLID BEACH PARK

THIS GATE OPEN 12 NOON
BEFORE 12 NOON GO TO BLVD. STAND GATE

(Illus. 218) The walkway along the bluffline overlooking the BEACH was once known as "LOVER'S LANE". This picture was taken on the last day of the final season, September 28, 1969. The fall clouds and lake's rough water with the distant downtown skyline present a forlorn vista.

(Don Woods Collection)

(Illus. 219) OVER-THE-FALLS: a 35-foot, 35-degree scream.

(Illus. 220) The steep descent that followed this ascent of OVER-THE-FALLS sometimes left an impression on the stomach.

(Don Woods Collection)

(Illus. 221) The dousing at OVER-THE-FALLS never dampened spirits.

(Michael A. Fuerst Collection)

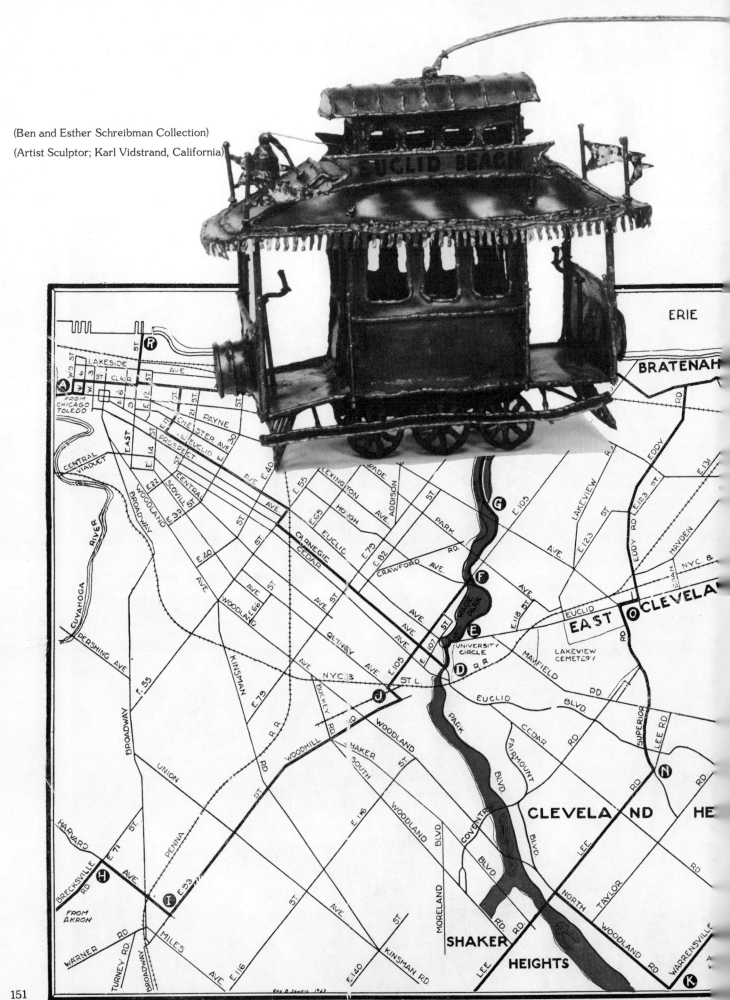

(Ben and Esther Schreibman Collection)

(Artist Sculptor; Karl Vidstrand, California)

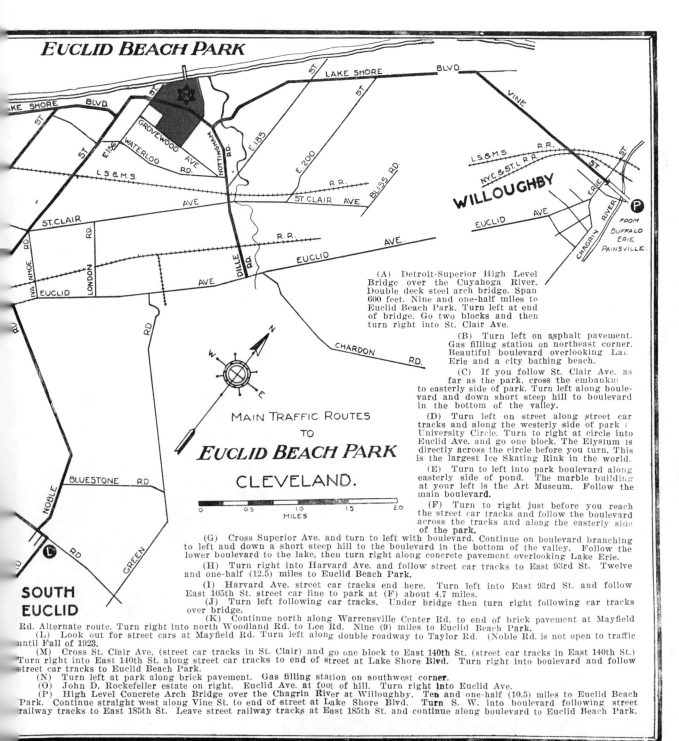

EUCLID BEACH PARK

LAKE SHORE BLVD.

WILLOUGHBY

MAIN TRAFFIC ROUTES
TO
EUCLID BEACH PARK
CLEVELAND.

SOUTH EUCLID

(A) Detroit-Superior High Level Bridge over the Cuyahoga River. Double deck steel arch bridge. Span 600 feet. Nine and one-half miles to Euclid Beach Park. Turn left at end of bridge. Go two blocks and then turn right into St. Clair Ave.

(B) Turn left on asphalt pavement. Gas filling station on northeast corner. Beautiful boulevard overlooking Lake Erie and a city bathing beach.

(C) If you follow St. Clair Ave. as far as the park, cross the embankment to easterly side of park. Turn left along boulevard and down short steep hill to boulevard in the bottom of the valley.

(D) Turn left on street along street car tracks and along the westerly side of park i University Circle. Turn to right at circle into Euclid Ave. and go one block. The Elysium is directly across the circle before you turn. This is the largest Ice Skating Rink in the world.

(E) Turn to left into park boulevard along easterly side of pond. The marble building at your left is the Art Museum. Follow the main boulevard.

(F) Turn to right just before you reach the street car tracks and follow the boulevard across the tracks and along the easterly side of the park.

(G) Cross Superior Ave. and turn to left with boulevard. Continue on boulevard branching to left and down a short steep hill to the boulevard in the bottom of the valley. Follow the lower boulevard to the lake, then turn right along concrete pavement overlooking Lake Erie.

(H) Turn right into Harvard Ave. and follow street car tracks to East 93rd St. Twelve and one-half (12.5) miles to Euclid Beach Park.

(I) Harvard Ave. street car tracks end here. Turn left into East 93rd St. and follow East 105th St. street car line to park at (F) about 4.7 miles.

(J) Turn left following car tracks. Under bridge then turn right following car tracks over bridge.

(K) Continue north along Warrensville Center Rd. to end of brick pavement at Mayfield Rd. Alternate route. Turn right into north Woodland Rd. to Lee Rd. Nine (9) miles to Euclid Beach Park.

(L) Look out for street cars at Mayfield Rd. Turn left along double roadway to Taylor Rd. (Noble Rd. is not open to traffic until Fall of 1923.

(M) Cross St. Clair Ave. (street car tracks in St. Clair) and go one block to East 140th St. (street car tracks in East 140th St.) Turn right into East 140th St. along street car tracks to end of street at Lake Shore Blvd. Turn right into boulevard and follow street car tracks to Euclid Beach Park.

(N) Turn left at park along brick pavement. Gas filling station on southwest corner.

(O) John D. Rockefeller estate on right. Euclid Ave. at foot of hill. Turn right into Euclid Ave.

(P) High Level Concrete Arch Bridge over the Chagrin River at Willoughby. Ten and one-half (10.5) miles to Euclid Beach Park. Continue straight west along Vine St. to end of street at Lake Shore Blvd. Turn S. W. into boulevard following street railway tracks to East 185th St. Leave street railway tracks at East 185th St. and continue along boulevard to Euclid Beach Park.

152

(Edward C. Chukayne Collection)

(Illus. 224) A park bench, some POPCORN and the afternoon sun.

(Michael A. Fuerst Collection)

(Illus. 223) Euclid Beach was a park that you could just sit and enjoy.

(Michael A. Fuerst Collection)

(Illus. 225) Snow covered benches by the OUTDOOR BANDSTAND wait for spring.

(Russell Allon Hehr Collection

(Illus. 226)

(Illus. 227) The final stretch of the RACING COASTER.

(Illus. 226, 227, 228) The ever popular RACING
COASTER—until September, 1969.

(Illus. 228) The first hill ascent of the RACING COASTER.

(Michael A. Fuerst Collection)

156

(Illus. 229) Covered walkways were a basic part of the beach.

(Michael A. Fuerst Collection)

(Illus. 230) The majestic ROCKET SHIPS could take you anywhere your imagination wished.

(Michael A. Fuerst Collection)

(Illus. 231) There was nothing like a quick and cooling drink of water as busy visitors rushed from ride to ride.

(William Stoneback Collection)

(Illus. 231a) This area of the promenade was an outdoor bandstand for
a short period during the 1920s.

(Michael A. Fuerst Collection)

(Illus. 232)

(Collections of Richard C. Walter, Jeff Mach, Robert Cigoy, Lynn Velesko, Cindy Swearinger and Ed Chukayne)

160

(Don Woods Collection)   (Illus. 233) COASTER profile.

(Illus. 234) As if airborne, this rider puts his FLYING SCOOTER through its paces.

(Tom Satyrshur Collection)

(Illus. 235) The gleaming ROCKET SHIPS, the music of the band organ, rustling trees and lake breezes were basic to any memory of Euclid Beach.

(Tom Satyrshur Collection)

(Illus. 236)

(Illus. 238)

(Illus. 236, 237, 238) The endless shapes and designs produced by the intermingling of the various hills of the wooden roller coaster were intriguing. Three photos by Harry Luikart demonstrate the visual interest of the THRILLER and RACING COASTER structures.

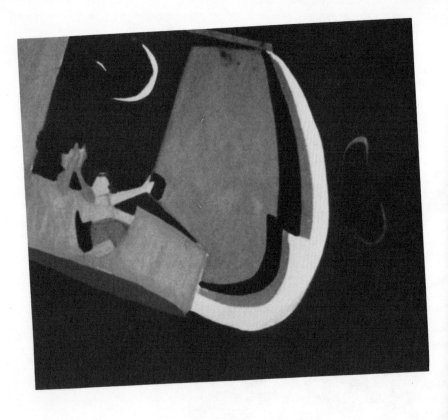

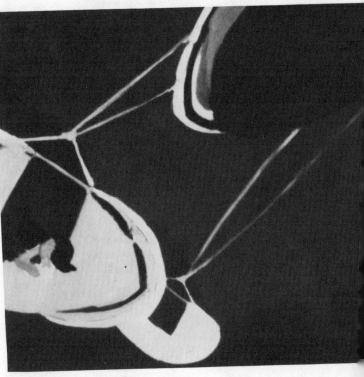

(Illus. 239) Four paintings of the FLYING
SCOOTERS by Neva Hansen.

(Illus. 240) Three paintings of horses that were on the CARROUSEL by Al Phillips.

(Harry Luikart Collection)

(Illus. 241) "Don't shoot until you see the" gleam of the electric light. The PENNY AR-CADE at Euclid Beach was small but packed with many enjoyable challenges.

(Illus. 242) The "Iron Claw" did not always co-operate in selecting the desired treasure.

(Michael A. Fuerst Collection)

(Illus. 243) Even though the GRANDMOTHER might advise visitors about another fortune all who came were fortunate.

(Michael A. Fuerst Collection)

(Illus. 244) "No. 1 Grove Avenue, Euclid Beach Park, Cleveland, Ohio" is the simple title of this painting; the house was typical of those occupied by the full-time employees of the park.

(Charles P. Wanda Collection)

GRAY SKIES CAST ON FALL

No popcorn balls were being sold today
I had to use my mind to sail away
Into a time when voices filled the air
Into the realm of what was yesterday.

Here lie the ghosts of life another way
When I arrived the ghosts came out to play
The greased-wood smell, the cars or just
      my mind
Remembering good times like nickle day.

  To see the things that
  use to mean so much
  To see them knowing
  they won't be seen again.

  When ever I hear the winds mournful call
  I'll always remember these gray skies
  cast on fall.

All of the rides had music they would play
The funhouse lady laughed step right this way
and all the screams of kids on coaster rides
would mistify the night and cheer the day.

  Where ever there are
  People who feel deep
  Memories in their life
  The living through it all.

  If you look closely
  I'm sure that you'll see
  The tears they're hiding
  Their gray skies cast on fall.

It all was there against a sky of gray
Most of the rides in piled rubble lay
Torn down, burnt down or standing to decay
But as I left it seemed there was a voice
A voice saying taffy popcorn balls do not delay.

Steven Lee McBride
1972

167

(Illus. 245) The PIER provided a romantic setting for many. From the end of the PIER the park seemed to float in the night, aglow with thousands of lights, with many of the sounds muted by the waves meeting the BEACH. This reminiscence was painted by Charles P. Wanda.

(Charles P. Wanda Collection)

 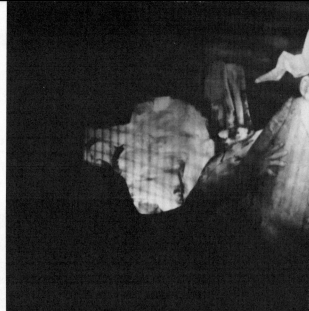

(Illus. 246) Two surprises furnished by the SURPRISE HOUSE were this fantastic spider, and these whistling boys. "Watch out for the snake around the corner."

(Don Woods Collection)

(Illus. 247) Watching the "laughing lady" LAUGHING SAL. She made a frightening impression on some.

(Michael A. Fuerst Collection)

(Illus. 248) The THRILLER:
maker of impressions on the
stomach. "All aboard!"

(Illus. 249)

(Carolyn E. Chukayne, Mrs. B. Donajtis, Steffie Kapel, Robert Lupton, Norm and Jim Worgull, Earl Tonkin and Robert Cigoy—all contributors)

(Illus. 249) Souvenirs of the past here include two Skee Balls, brass popcorn ball molds, a link of the THRILL-ER'S lift chain . . . recognize any of the others?

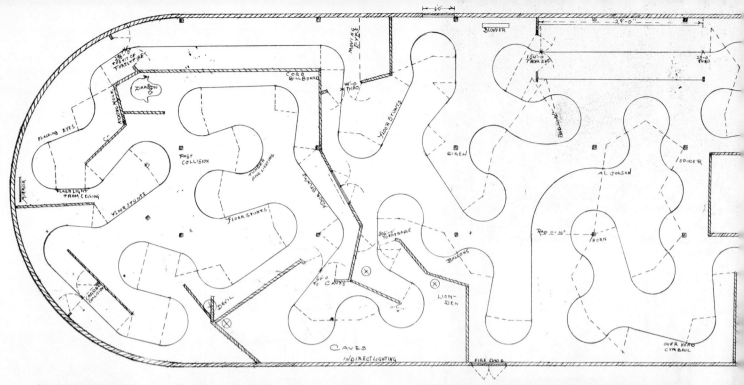

(Michael A. Fuerst Collection)

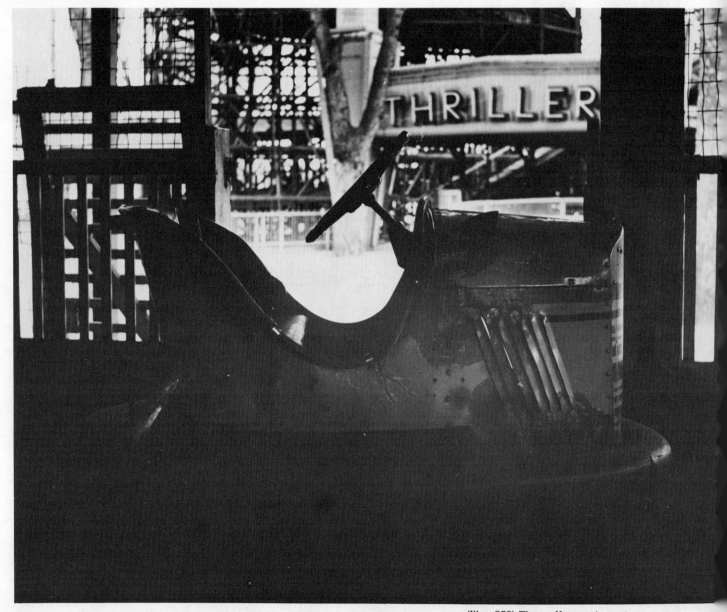

173

(Illus. 250) The traffic jam has sub-
sided—forever!

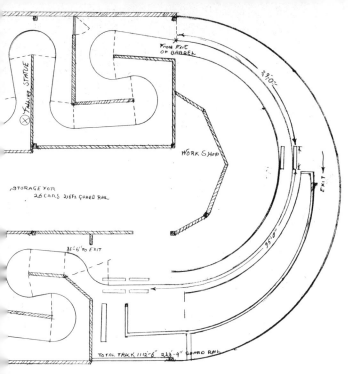

(Illus. 250-B) The LAFF-IN-THE-DARK left impressions on many people. The route of this "mysterious" ride can be traced on this plan.

(The Humphrey Company)

(Michael A. Fuerst Collection)

(Illus. 250A) Traffic was light on this day.

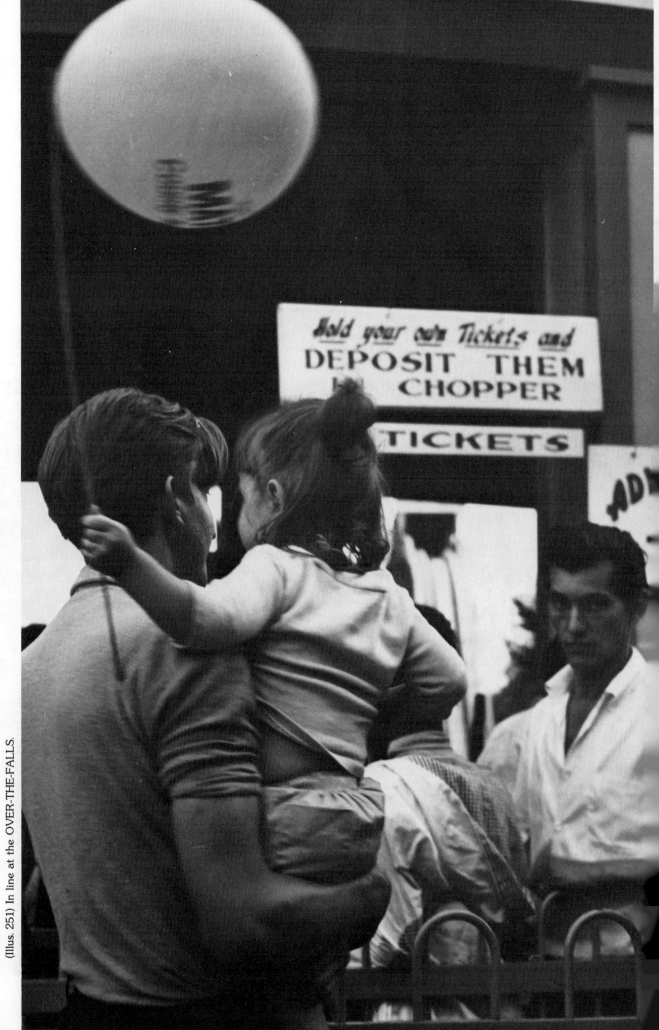

(Illus. 251) In line at the OVER-THE-FALLS.

DEPOSIT YOUR TICKETS

.NO REPEAT RIDES PLEASE

Through the '60s Euclid Beach aged just as a person might grey during a period of great stress. Although there was never any slackening of the high maintenance standards, the luster began to dull. Social patterns had changed and yet the mode of operation of Euclid Beach did not; it seemed that the two were incompatible. It was finally announced that the 1969 season would be the Beach's last. To many people it was incomprehensible.

Those who seek easy answers to difficult questions have already made their subjectively filtered assessment of the whys and wherefores of the park's closing. No discussion will alter these emotion-filled accusations. The disappearance of so many old parks through the '50s to the present suggests many and varied forces in cultural change at work, adjusting our values concerning the way in which we entertain ourselves.

Most of the approaches to the loading area of the rides at the Beach had a wooden walkway or ramp. The ramp was usually painted with grey deck paint. As the ticket chopper was passed, excitement grew. During many of the years of operation repeat rides were possible for one ticket less than the number required for the original trip. After the last ticket was deposited on September 28, 1969, there would be "no repeat rides, please."

(Illus. 252) Wide walkways and trees . . . the Beach.

(Harry Luikart Collection)

(Illus. 253) "Should we ride the THRILLER or the FLYING TURNS first?" The choice has been already made.

(Harry Luikart Collection)

(Illus. 254) A high point in experience—now leveled! The THRILLER.

(Harry Luikart Collection)

(Illus. 255) Even if only a few took the journey the trip was worth it.

(Harry Luikart Collection)

(Illus. 256) Too few were running from ride to ride in the last days.

(Harry Luikart Collection)

(Illus. 257) Shaded benches, numerous trees and covered walkways provided an almost serene setting at Euclid Beach.

(Russell Allon Hehr Collection)

(Illus. 258) Many a visitor to the park remembers the long covered walkway that left the bus stop (formerly a street car loading and unloading area). Its route led by the OVER-THE-FALLS, SLEEPY HOLLOW RAILROAD, and PONY RIDE into the COLONNADE and KIDDIELAND.

(William Stoneback Collection)

(Illus. 259) The walkway along the bluff overlooking the
BEACH was always pleasant, as this 1968 photo shows.

(Illus. 261) No patter of little feet. (Michael A. Fuerst Collection)

, 260) KIDDIELAND graffiti. A generation s its signature.

nael A. Fuerst Collection)

(Illus. 262) The leaves were among the last visitors to KIDDIELAND.

(Michael A. Fuerst Collection)

(Illus. 263) The incomporable FRO-ZEN WHIP. You can still enjoy it.

(Illus. 264) The PENNY ARCADE was always on the itinerary during a day's visit to Euclid Beach.

The sign on the gate reads:
THIS GATE OPEN.. 12 NOON
BEFORE 12 noon GO TO HRB. STAND GATE

(Illus. 266) There was no way out for Euclid Beach in 1969, but this 1956 picture shows the closed gates waiting for the next spring.

(Russell Allon Hehr Collection)

(Illus. 265) Turned away! The MAIN GATE is closed forever at Euclid Beach Park. These folks will never have another chance to come to the Beach.

(Michael A. Fuerst Collection)

(Illus. 267A) OVER-THE-FALLS brought a chilling experience to many, but yet, the setting remained peaceful. (1968)

191

(Illus. 267) Vandalism, with some extreme consequences, became a popular activity at the park after its close. This was the last "Surprise" at the SURPRISE HOUSE.

(Illus. 268) "LAUGHING SAL" de nude. Things got a little hot for Sal as a result of a 1961 fire in the SURPRISEHOUSE.

(Russell Allon Hehr Collection)

192

(Illus. 269) Unwelcome vistor.

(Michael A. Fuerst Collection)

(Illus. 270) Demise! The RACING COASTER would race no more.

(Russell Allon Hehr Collection)

(Illus. 271) No summer excursion boat will dock here. The PIER has been reclaimed by Lake Erie.

"SNOW ON THE CAROUSEL"

BY: LEE O. BUSH

THEME AND FANTASY FOR FLUTE AND GUITAR
BASED ON A SONG BY   LEE O. BUSH

SLOW AND STEADILY

SOME FUTURE THOUGHTS ON THE PAST — *A Post Script*

No medium can completely translate the unique charm and attendant universal appeal of a place like Euclid Beach Park or any other so-called "traditional" amusement park. The progress of time is almost inscrutable, much like observing a blade of grass growing. During a seemingly endless parade of summers the Beach persisted and flourished with a Gibralter-like constancy. Then, before we could rub our eyes clear, the park was gone as if it had never really existed.

The dull faded green, the peeling sycamores, the refreshing breezes that accompanied soft yellow-lit nights, the very feel of the place, all these seem more distant than the Ice Age. In a time of "present shock" where much of life is staged in a kind of combat zone, decorated with all things plastic, the contrast with the decade-distant Euclid Beach moments exceeds our imaginations. The imagination is an organ that is pursuing atrophy at an alarming rate and has almost ceased to serve us with the nourishment that the creative sense in each of us needs. We now go to an "amusing park" and watch, watch a movie or, in some other explicit terms, are spoon-fed entertainment. Such was not a necessity at Euclid Beach. True, there were movies there, but that was in an era when the imagination was an organ essential in perceiving the nature of the images on the screen. Now the "live" people seem more mechanized than the amusement devices.

ᴀᴢᴛᴇᴄ® FT – 8 R   DIAZ-TEC 800

Some people have said that if Euclid Beach Park had survived into the theme park "rejuvenation era," it would now be flourishing. Others simply dismiss that as wishful thinking. Whatever the case, something wedged deep within numerous generations seemed to *need* what the Beach had to offer. There also seems to be an unutterable sense of loss of that "something" within both persons who knew the park and those who never even set foot on the acreage. One might speculate about what it was that Euclid Beach satisfied: to provide carefree enjoyment, to supply a psychological salve, to furnish an illuminating experience or to hint of a Divine gift. One immutable fact is that literally millions of people miss the grand old place, and nowhere does a substitute seem evident.

Euclid Beach Park *is* closed for the season, *all* seasons, even after a second look. But, no matter how many probes take place through photos, drawings, words, and remembered experiences, a void persists in haunting those who would look twice or more. For those of us who have lost the Beach, let us learn to appreciate all that is of value; to those with a place like the Beach yet surviving, guard it; preserve it; patronize it; it is irreplaceable!

AMUSEMENT PARK BOOKS, Inc.
Lee O. Bush
Edward C. Chukayne
Russell Allon Hehr
Richard F. Hershey
September, 1979

BIBLIOGRAPHY

The major bibliography for BOTH volumes is on pages 301-305 in the FIRST volume EUCLID BEACH PARK IS CLOSED FOR THE SEASON. No duplication of entries in volume one appears in this second bibliography. Only additional material that has come to the authors' attention since the publication of the first volume is cited here. Also, audio visual material such as films, tapes and phonodiscs (records) are listed. Several references appearing in this bibliography are indirectly relevant; for completeness and for enthusiasts they have been included. Tapes and records appearing in the bibliography also appear in a separate list at the end of the bibliography.

B and N Productions. *TAPES OF THE SOUNDS OF EUCLID BEACH PARK*. Cleveland, Ohio: B and N Productions, 1978.

Berni Organ Co. *MECHANICAL BAND ORGANS*. New York, N. Y.: Berni Organ Company, 1913. (Reprinted by Vestal Press, Vestal, N. Y.)

Bishop, Robert. *AMERICAN FOLK SCULPTURE*. New York, N. Y.: E. P. Dutton & Co., Inc. 1974.

Braithwaite, David. *SAVAGE OF KINGS LYNN*. Cambridge: Patrick Stevens, 1975.

Carousel Productions. Record. THE GAVIOLI RECALLS EUCLID BEACH. Botsford, Conn.: Carousel Productions, n. d.

"Carousels." The Encyclopedia of Collectibles, volume 3. New York, N. Y.: Time-Life Books, 1978.

CAROUSEL ART. Garden Grove, California: Marge Swenson. Quarterly, 1978.

Christensen, Erwin O. *EARLY AMERICAN WOOD CARVING*. Cleveland and N. Y.: World Publishing Co., 1952.

Concert Recording [Co.]. Record. *AMERICA 1900*. CR MO53. Lynwood, California, n. d.

E. Boecker Organ and Orchestrion Co. *CATALOG*. New York, N. Y.: Boecker Organ and Orchestrion Co. n. d.

Flint, Richard. *RESEARCH GUIDE TO AMUSEMENT RIDES, PARKS, FAIRS and CARNIVALS*. (unpublished book)

Fraley, Nina. *THE AMERICAN CAROUSEL*. Berkeley, California: Redbug Workshop, 1979.

Fried, Frederick. *ARTISTS IN WOOD*. New York, N. Y.: Clarkson, N. Potter, Inc., 1970.

Fried, Frederick. "Last Ride for Carousel Figures?" *HISTORIC PRESERVATION*, July-September, 1977.

Fried, Frederick and Mary. *AMERICA'S FORGOTTEN FOLK ARTS*. New York, N. Y.: Pantheon Books, 1978.

G. Molinari & Sons. *CAROUSEL ORGANS*. New York, N. Y.: G. Molinari & Sons, 1896 (also reprinted by Vestal Press, Vestal, N. Y.)

Gottdenker, Tina Cristiani. *CARVERS AND THEIR MERRY-GO-ROUNDS*. West Babylon, N. Y.: Second Annual Conference Committee, National Carousel Roundtable, 1974.

Horning, Clarence P. *TREASURY OF AMERICAN DESIGN*. New York, N. Y.: Harry N. Abrams, Inc. 1967. 2 Vols.

"Horsing Around: Carousels On the Comeback." *DISCOVERY*, Summer, 1979.

Hunter, Susan. *A FAMILY GUIDE TO AMUSEMENT CENTERS*. New York, N. Y.: Walker and Company, 1975.

Ilyinsky, Paul. *GOODBYE, CONEY ISLAND, GOODBYE*. Englewood Cliffs, New Jersey: Prentice-Hall, 1972.

Kasson, John F. *AMUSING THE MILLION*. New York, N. Y.: Hill and Wang, 1978.

Lawson, Robert. *THE GREAT WHEEL*. New York, N. Y.: Viking Press, 1957.

Lipman, Jean. *AMERICAN FOLK ART IN WOOD, METAL AND STONE*. New York, N. Y.: Pantheon Books, 1948.

Margaret Woodbury, Strong Museum. *STEP RIGHT UP!*, Rochester, New York: Margaret Woodbury Strong Museum, 1977.

MERRY-GO-ROUNDUP. National Carousel Association. Quarterly, 1974 —.

Onosko, Tim. *FUN LAND, U. S. A.* New York, N. Y.: Ballantine Books, 1978.

Peerless Record Co., Ltd.: Record, (2 record album). *GAVIOLI MUSICAL CIRCUS*. Stereo D T 015. Brentford, England: Peerless Record Co. Ltd., n. d.

—, Record, (2 volumes). *110 KEY GAVIOLI FAIR ORGAN*. DE 1018, DE 1017, —, n. d.

Reed, James W. *THE TOP 100 AMUSEMENT PARKS OF THE UNITED STATES*. Quarryville, Pa.: Reed Publishing Co., 1978.

Scott, David. Films. *FILMS TAKEN OF EUCLID BEACH PARK BY DUDLEY HUMPHREY SCOTT.* Various dates.

Summit, Roland. *FLYING HORSES*. Rolling Hills, California: Flying Horses, 1970.

W. F. Mangels Co. Carousel Works. *CATALOGUE NO. 4,* Coney Island, N. Y.: W. F. Mangels Co., n. d. (also reprinted by Early Times Catalogues, Rapid City, South Dakota: Fenwyn Press, Inc. 1969).

Waldrop, John, Richard Munch, Jon-Michael Reed. *ROLLER COASTER FEVER*. New York, N. Y.: Starlog Press, 1979.

Westbrook, Bill and Thomas Hale. *WHERE HAVE ALL THE HORSES GONE.* Richmond, Virginia: Westover Publishing Co., 1973.

Wickens, Richard. *CAROUSELS IN OHIO.* Cleveland, Ohio: Privately Printed, 1978.

Wlodarczyk, Chuck. *RIVERVIEW: GONE BUT NOT FORGOTTEN, 1904-1967.* Evanston, Illinois: The Schori Press, 1977.

RECORDS AND TAPES OF THE SOUNDS OF EUCLID BEACH PARK.

B and N Productions. *TAPES OF THE SOUNDS OF EUCLID BEACH PARK.* Cleveland, Ohio: B and N Productions, 1978.

—. Record, (2 Volumes). *110 KEY GAVIOLI FAIR ORGAN.* DE 1018, DE 1017, —, n. d.

Concert Recording [Co.]. Record. *AMERICA 1900.* CR MO53. Lynwood, Calif., n. d.

Peerless Record Co., Ltd. Record, (2 record albums). *GAVIOLI MUSICAL CIRCUS.* Stereo DI 015. Brentford, England: Peerless Record Co., Ltd., n. d.

Carousel Productions. Record. *THE GAVIOLI RECALLS EUCLID BEACH.* Botsford, Conn.: Carousel Products, n. d.

EUCLID BEACH EMPLOYEES ROSTER

APPENDIX A

A Representative List, Not Complete

Al Abbey
Al Abby
Phyllis Agresta
George Albright
Irene Andersen
Paul L. Andersen
Mrs. J. A. Anderson
Jack Anderson
John Anderson
Harry L. Arnold
W. Atkins
Ernest J. Attwood
Ed Austin
Alice Baber
Olin A. Bailey
Don Baldwin
Frank Baldwin
Harold Baldwin
Joe Baldwin
Howard Bales
Robert Barbo
Norman Bargholt
Roland Barhyte
Frank Barkerio
E. Barney
Henry Barnhardt
J. T. Barry
David W. Bauer
B. Bayne
Clarence Beam
Ed Beamer
Roger J. Behra
Jim Behrend
Elton Beil
Rob F. Berlan
Ken Bernhardt
Lenny Black
Bernice Blatnik
Bill Blauty
Philip Blehete
Burt C. Bliss
Dr. R. S. Bodenstein
Brian T. Bonjack
D. Bowle
Bob Boyce
Ken Boyce
Robert Boyle
Zavrence R. Brahs
W. Braidey
Jean Brass
  (nee Clatterbuck)
Dolores Breidenbach
Clarence Brennen
Dan Brennan
Wm. Brennan
Walter Briggs
J. C. Bright
Charles Britton
Frank Brodnick
Jack Brown

Orr Brown
Peter Brugo
Thomas E. Bryant
Ray Buell
Sara Stoneback
  Bundus
Arnold W. Burger
Dorothy Burke
  (nee Baker)
Patrick Burke
Otto Burkhardt
Tom Burns
James Burton
Elsie Buzzelli
Robert J. Cahill
H. Caldwell
Robert C. Callaghan
Donna Campbell
Julian E. Carlisle
L. J. Carroll
Thomas Carson
W. B. Carter
Frank A. Catalano
Vincent C. Catalano
Jack Cawan
Edward Cetina
Carol Chamberlain
Matilda Chamberlain
  (nee Kastelic)
Peter Cheepman
Cyril Chinn
Pat Cirino
Charles B. Clarke
Eberly Clayton
R. Clegg
Kevin Coleman
Lloyd Collier
Edward Collins
Gary Conrad
Linda Conrad
Tom Conry
Norman S. Cook
Larry Cooley
Ray Critzer
John Cross
Grace R. Curtis
Muriel Cyrgalis
Charles Dalton
Paul V. Daugherty
Richard C. Daunegger
M. Davie
Russell Davies
Charles E. Davis
W. Davis
Allene Daw
O'Dell Dean
Harvey Decker
Domonic Delembo
Frank Delembo
Lloyd Denman

T. J. Denman
Geo. E. Dennison
Bertha Devoe
Archibald Dick
Robert Dietrich
Ronald P. Dietz
L. W. Dill
Tommy Dinnalia
Donald D. Ditto
Stanley Dlugoleski
Adele Dollard
Steve Dossa
Robert Dowd
Bob Downey, Jr.
M. Downing
Joseph Dragonetti
Hariet Weber Dressler
Jack H. Dressler
Jim Dryburgh
Wesley Dwyer
Bole Edwardsen
Tom Egan
Walter K. Elbrecht
Louise Eldridge
John Elish
Frank England
S. England
Molly Tomaric Evans
Dorothy Ewald
Anthony J. Ezzo
Herby J. Fallas
John Farley
Arthur Faulker
Earl Fernal
C. Ferrel
Ada Fier
Frank Fier
Avery Finger
Ed Fisher
Helen Fitzgerald
Elmer Fletcher
Jessie Fletterich
Martin Fletterich
Gen Fogarty
R. E. Forgason
Sue Formick
George Fox
Winifred Francis
John Francis
G. Freeman
Norman Freeman
James J. Friel
A. W. Fritz
Fred Furze
Henry Fussner
William Fussner
Dan H. Galbraith
Edmond Gallon, Jr.
William J. Gannet
Max Gast

C. Gent
William Gent, Jr.
William Gent, Sr.
Violet Gipson
  (nee Durkin)
Donald W. Gliebo
Henry Gogolin
Ken Goldberg
E. Goldburg
Neil Grdolnik
Fred Greenway
Edward Griffith
Art Gronert
N. W. Grossman, Sr.
Charles Guhde
Don Guhde
John Guthrie
Harold Guy
Flo Hack
Roger Hack
S. Haines
R. Hagedorn
C. H. Hallwood
Robert C. Halterman
O. Hanchett
Dick Hanzel
Gertrude Hardy
Harry Harnhardt
George Harris
Bob Hassett
Robert A. Heckman
Alice H. Heidt
J. M. Heidt
D. C. Heitman
Norma Heitman
W. Hendershot
C. Herrick
George R. Herwood
Henry Hess
E. Hickock
Roy Hickox
Gottleib Hirsch
Tom Hirsch
N. H. Hirter
Harvey W. Hock
Harvey Hoffmer
F. Hogne
C. Holtz
John J. Hopkins
Mrs. L. M. Hormel
William Hradisky
Edward P. Hudson
Sara Huffman
David H. Humphrey
Dudley S. Humphrey II
Dudley S. Humphrey III
Effie D. Humphrey
  (nee Shannon)
H. Louise Humphrey
Harlow Humphrey

Harvey J. Humphrey
Kathryn Humphrey
Linnie Humphrey
Dorothy M. Hunt
Scott Hunt
Clarence Hunter
James Hussy
W. Huyat
Al Jacklitz
Robert Jennings
Frank J. Jeran
Cliff B. Johnson
Don Johnson
Ed Johnson
James Johnson
Norm Johnson
S. B. Johnson
W. F. Johnston
Donald Jones
J. Jones
Rose Jones
George Joseph
"Es" Judd
R. Kagin
Frank Kamm
  (Kaminskas)
Betty Kane
  (nee Slusser)
Helen Kaselak
Dale Kast
Howard Kast
Robert E. Kast
Frank Kastelic
Helen Kazelak
Wm. Keegan
Marge Kekic
J. V. Kelly
Arthur R. Kennedy
Edward C. Kent
Ted Kent
Bary Kern
Jack H. Kidd
Harry Kidwell
Frank Kilby
Mabel Killaly
  (nee Humphrey)
Pierce Killaly
Jack Kimbel
Jim Kinzer
Robert K. Kirchner
Gale Kirts
Ruth Klassen
P. J. Knight
John Kobie
John F. Koble
Bill Koeing
Marie Kolesar
Charlie Koons
Mary Kostelnik
  (nee Clifford)

203

During the 75 years of its existence, thousands of people were employed at E.B.P. Unfortunately, the task of locating and listing all of them would be monumental, so we were able to include only a fraction of that number.

This partial listing of former employees was compiled at various mall shows and other events where people proudly informed the authors of their early employment. A reunion group of former Humphrey Co. employees is planned with events to take place at Shady Lake Park. For further information contact one of the authors.

Paul J. Kostura
Jane Kramer
Dorothy Krause
G. Krause
Harry Krause
F. R. Kreger
Kathryn Kubelavic
Peter Kubelavic
W. Kuhlman
Fred Kupfer
Fred M. Kushen
Jack Lambie
Louise Lambie
   (nee Humphrey)
A. Lance
Elmer Land
Clark Lape
Pete Lasco
Joseph Jas. Laurich
Harvey Lawson
Marie Leece
Robert Leetch
Bunny Lemieux
Archie Lerick
Harry Lerick
Arthur Lersich
Lottie Lesher
Betty Leslie
Chas. J. Leuenberger
Frank A. Levar
David C. Lewis
William Light
Vance Linamen
Fred D. Lipp
George Lister
Ben D. Lukas
Bob Lupton
Ruth M. Lupton
Jeanette Lust
Jim Lylie
Joe Lylie
A. MacDonald
John MacDonald
Olie MacElrath
Doris Mackley
   (nee Humphrey)
Dan Macko
William J. Maclevie
Ida A. Magner
Ida Maler
Mrs. Mallios
Daniel Mallory
Margaret Mallory
   (nee Lechowicz)
John Malner
Bill Malourh
Leslie Mandau
Rudy Mandau
Dan Manning
Don L. Manning

Douglas L. Manning
Helen Manning
Dorothy Mapstone
Dominic Marino
Chris Marshall
Lester Marshall
Luther Martin
Ronald Martin
Louise A. Matias
Holly Maurer
   (nee Lupton)
Joseph Mazzolini
Lambert McCauley
W. J. McClevie
Kenneth N. McClintock
R. McCoy
Angelina McDonald
Nettie McGregor
Charles McHale
"Doc" McIlrath
David McKnight
Helene McPherson
John Means
Harry Mechtensimer
Edward Medves
Paul Mercer
Christian Meurer
Stephen Mika
Steve Miljenovic
Al Miller
Dee Miller
Ladeema Miller
Locke Miller
Neil Miller
Russell Miller
Walter Miller
Wayne E. Mills
Roy Mizner
Eugene A. Molle
Robert A. Molle
E. Monroe
Judy Kekic Moodry
Ed S. Moore
Alva Morrow
Ernest D. Morrow
Hugh J. Morgan
Mike Mower
Dick Muckel
A. Muller
Dick Mullen
Jake Mullen
John Murphey
E. Murphy
Dorothy Murphy
John Murrachak
B. Murray
James Murray
Kathryn Murray
R. E. Murray
John Nalbach

Fred Nelson
Bob Nolan
Mickey Nolan
Lawrence Oberdank
Jim O'Connor
Theodore Okowski
Walter Okowski
William O'Neil
Caroline Opalk
Martin Opalk
Kenneth Othberg
R. Z. Owen
Gene Padden
John Palmer
John Pappaleo
Donald M. Park
Bill Parker
Henry C. Parker
Erie Patchin
R. Paton
R. A. Pease
Kenneth Peck
Lois Peck
Freida Pecon
Rudy Pegoraro
A. Percell
B. Perkins
Charles Persell
Enos Peterson, Jr.
Enos S. Peterson, Sr.
Daniel Petrick
Clarence Philpott
Pat Pillar (nee Kekic)
H. Poland
Norman Poland
Tom Polland
Vincent E. Powell
Anne Prekel
Henry Prekel
F. L. Price
Otto Price
Ralph Price
John J. Primeau
James Pulner
Marge Purdy
Robert G. Pustare
Kenneth W. Puttman
Russ Ramsey
William A. Raupach
Edward A. Reardon
Roger Reardon
O. Redmond
George Reinhard, Jr.
George Reinhard, Sr.
Rob Reinke
Donald A. Ressler
C. F. Riblet
S. I. Riblet
Billie Richards
Chester Richards

Gilbert Rider
Larry Riga
Mike Rinderle
Frank Ritchie
Jim Robinson
Pearl Robinson
E. Romanis
Neil Rozum
Louis A. Ruscitto
T. B. Rutherford
Alan Ryan
Alice Ryel
R. Sampson
W. Sasager
Alice M. Sator
Mike Scarl
Paul Schad
Emma Schaefer
Barbara Schedler
Kenneth C. Schedler
Roland W. Schedler
William Schellentrager
Augie Schill
Grace Schinall
Kenneth Schoenbeck
Pauline Schoenbeck
Alfred K. Schoenbera
Al Schuessler
Carol Scott
David Scott
Dudley H. Scott
Louise Scott
Marion Scott
L. W. Scutt
Ben Seaman, Sr.
A. Sefquist
Ed Selia
John Selmer
Ernest Shandle
Harry Shannon
Ralph Shedden
James Sheehan
Frank Sherwood
Everrett Shilliday
Kathryn Shilliday
   (nee Greenland)
Betty Shirer
Joseph Shively
Juanita Sinko
H. Skelly
Thomas Skelly
Rudalph F. Skerl
Anthony Skubic
Joe Skur
R. Smekel
Alan H. Smith
Albert Smith
Charles L. Smith
Chas. Smith
Clifford Smith

Donald D. Smith
Edna Smith
   (nee Jackson)
Florence Smith
Herman Smith
Josie Smith
Mildred E. Smith
Robert Smith
George Snyder
Joseph Squires
Betty Sojeba
H. Stanbury
Ord. Standfield
Asp. Stanley
Art Steele
Elsie Steele
Richard Steele
Harry Stellar
Harry Steller
Norma Stelter
   (nee Ellis)
Frank Stewart
James Stih
Howard Stoneback
John Stoneback
William H. Stoneback
Clint Storms
F. Storms
Mary Stringer
Wilferd E. Strodtbeck
Harry W. Stroud
Eugene Stuart
John Stuart
Mindy Stuart
Dick Stuck
N. Sullivan
O. P. Sutton
Wm. C. Swackhamer
David Swank
Angela Sweeny
John Sweeny
Julius Szuhy
Tom Tann
Josephine R. Tate
Arthur W. Taylor
Norman Tegun
J. E. Tennant
Bob Terrell
William Terrett
Ray Thomas
John Thompson
Mildred Thompson
   (nee Colarik)
Ted Thompson
Wm. Thompson Tinck
Ed Tisher
Joseph Tomsic
Carmen Tranchito
May Treter
Carlton Truman

Continued on Page 207   (Harry Luikart Collection)   204

RIDE BIOGRAPHY

APPENDIX B

Ride	Seasons at Euclid Beach	Fate or Destination
AERO DIPS	1909-1964	razed
ANTIQUE AUTOS	1964-1969	Shady Lake Park
AUTO TRAIN	c1901-1969	community of Mayfield Village, Ohio
BOUBLE BOUNCE	1939-1956	Lake Pontchartrain, New Orleans, then to Seattle's World Fair, 1962
BUG	c1928-1969	Geauga Lake Park, Aurora, Ohio (cars only—used for parts)
CARROUSEL (PTC #9)	1905-1909	Laurel Springs, Connecticut
CARROUSEL (PTC #19)	1910-1969	Old Orchard Beach, Maine
CATERPILLAR	? -c1928	dismantled
COFFEE BREAK	1966-1969	Shady Lake Park
DIPPY WHIP	1938-1965	dismantled and sold
DODGEM	1921-1969	Shady Lake Park
FERRIS WHEEL	1896-1901	dismantled
FERRIS WHEEL	1965-1969	Shady Lake Park
FIGURE EIGHT	1904-1909	dismantled
FLYING PONIES	1903-c1934	reported to be moved to Rye Beach, N.Y.
FLYING SCOOTERS	1930-1969	Shady Lake Park
FLYING TURNS	1930-1969	razed
GREAT AMERICAN RACING DERBY	1921-1965	Cedar Point, Sandusky, Ohio
HAUNTED SWING	pre-1900	dismantled
HURRICANE	1960's	dismantled and sold
KIDDIELAND		Shady Lake Park (most rides)
LAFF-IN-THE-DARK	1931-1969	razed
MERRY-GO-ROUND	1896-1904	dismantled and sold
MILL CHUTE	1921-1936	redesigned to become OVER-THE-FALLS
OCEAN WAVE	early 1900's	dismantled
OVER-THE-FALLS	1937-1969	razed
RACING COASTER	1913-1969	razed
RED BUG BOULEVARD	mid-1930's	dismantled
ROCK-O-PLANE	1950's	dismantled and sold
ROCKET SHIPS (CIRCLE SWING)	1902-1969	razed
ROTOR	1957-1969	Shady Lake Park
SCENIC RAILWAY	1907-1936	dismantled
SCRAMBLER	mid-1960's-1969	Shady Lake Park
SLEEPY HOLLOW RAILROAD	early 1900's-1969	Shady Lake Park
SURPRISE HOUSE	1935-1969	razed
SWINGIN' GYMS	1964-1969	dismantled and sold
SWITCHBACK RAILWAY	1896-1903	dismantled
THRILLER	1924-1969	razed
TILT-A-WHIRL	1966-1969	Shady Lake Park
TURNPIKE	1962-1969	Shady Lake Park
WHIP	c1915-1936	dismantled
WITCHING WAVES	late 1920's-1930	converted to LAFF-IN-THE-DARK
ZOOMER	late 1920's-1930	dismantled

The Humphrey Popcorn, Popcorn Balls, Candy Kisses and Frozen Whip can still be enjoyed at Shady Lake Park, Streetsboro, Ohio.

Six views of the PTC CARROUSEL #19 now (1979) at Old Orchard Beach, Maine.

(Richard Wickens Collection)

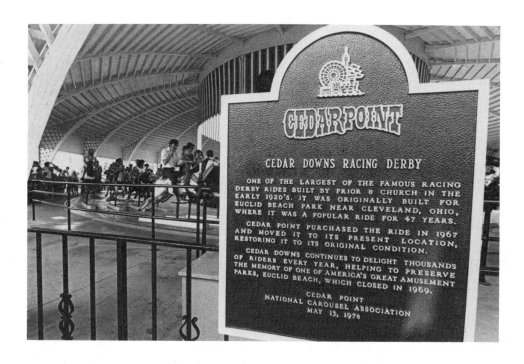

Prior and Church's GREAT AMERICAN RACING DERBY became CEDAR DOWNS when it was moved to Cedar Point, Sandusky, Ohio.

(Cedar Point)

(Photographs by Dan Feicht and Bob Stern)

APPENDIX C

ADDENDUM
ANNUALS, PICNICS, SHOWS, EVENTS, OUTINGS AT EUCLID BEACH PARK

Buckeye Forging
C.R.O.V.A.E.A.
Chase Brass and Copper Co.
Communication Workers
Diamond Alkali
Electrical Workers, Local #38
Ford Stamping Plant
Forest City Foundries
Forest City Materials
Gabriel Company
Inland Steel
Mechanics Educational Society
of America, Local 19
Meyer Dairy Products Co.
National Management Club
Park Synagogue
Parmatown
Salvation Army
Sugardale Hot Dog Day
Tip Top Bakeries
United Hungarian Societies
Warner & Swasey

(Parmadale Collection)

Employees Roster
Continued from Page 204

Ralph Trunkey	Jim Walker	Harry Watson	Walter Williams	Lester Wolff
Robert W. Tunquist	John E. Walter	Budd Webb	William Williams	Frank Wood
Ed VanHoate	Josephine Walter	George Webber	Kenneth G. Willis	Peter Wood
George VanHoate	Kitty O'Connor Walter	George Weber	Bud Wilson	Don Woods
Howard VanSchoor	J. E. Walters	Richard L. Weber	Dick Wilson	E. J. Woolmington
L. Vaughn	Alta Wanda	Clarence Weiner	George Wilson	David Wretschko
Gene Vehr	Charles P. Wanda	J. Whitehead	George L. Wilson	Andy Yaho
Bob "Bugs" Vogel	Homer Ward	George Wilcox	George W. Wilson	J. J. Yeager
Gary Vogrin	Robert Ward	Arthur A. Will	Robert O. Wilson	Carl Zanzig
Mary VonAlt	Paul E. Warren	Karl Will	Donald E. Winkle	Frank Zgontz
Herbert Wachsman	Ray Wasniak	Grace Williams	James R. Wise	Al DiLiberto
H. D. Walker	W. Watkins	Rhoda Williams	Melvin E. Wise	John Takacs
				Lou Takacs

INDEX

VOLUME ONE
EUCLID BEACH PARK
"is closed for the season"

FROM A.S.C.A.P. TO ZOOMER

Some notes for the reader using this index:

1. The contraction EBP refers to EUCLID BEACH PARK.
2. All MAP numbers cited are keyed to the numbers on the map on pp. 189 and 190.
3. All Illus. numbers are preceded by page numbers, e.g., Illus., p. 5 #6.
4. The order followed under each MAJOR HEADING is:
   1.) Subheadings (may also refer to Illus. or MAP numbers.)
   2.) **Illus., In boldface.**
   3.) MAP, IN CAPS.
   4.) *See and/or See Also In italics.*

Volume 1

Volume 1

Volume 1

Volume 1

Volume 1

Volume 1

Volume 1

Volume 1

Volume 1

Volume 1

Volume 1

Volume 1

Volume 1

Volume 1

Volume 1

Volume 1

Volume 2

Some notes for the reader using this index:

1. The contraction EBP refers to EUCLID BEACH PARK.
2. All Illus. numbers are preceded by page numbers, e.g., Illus., p. 5 #6.
3. The order followed under each MAJOR HEADING is:
   1.) Subheadings (may also refer to Illus.)
   2.) **Illus., In boldface.**
   3.) *See and/or See Also In italics.*

INDEX

VOLUME TWO
EUCLID BEACH PARK
"A SECOND LOOK"

Volume 2

Volume 2

Volume 2

Your Personal Euclid Beach Memories

Book Composition
Typography
Body Copy — Souvenir, Souvenir Italic, Souvenir Medium
Headlines — Tiffany Heavy
By: Typesetting Service, Inc.
1104 Prospect Avenue
Cleveland, Ohio 44115

Lithoprinted by
Braun-Brumfield, Inc.
Ann Arbor, Michigan

Bring The Family

and Enjoy The Day With Your Neighbors

CITY OF EUCLID

COMMUNITY PICNIC

AT BEAUTIFUL

EUCLID BEACH PARK

THURSDAY

JUNE 11TH

AFTERNOON and EVENING

THOUSANDS OF FREE RIDES

On Park Amusements . . . For Young and Old

· Games · Races · Fun For All
FREE DRAWING FOR PRIZE at 8:30
STUBS FOR DRAWING AVAILABLE AT LOG CABIN HEADQUARTERS

Free Pop Concert
By
EUCLID CIVIC ORCHESTRA
Harry Hershey, Directing
EUCLID CIVIC CHORUS
Kenneth Nash, Directing
7:30 - 8:30
MAIN DANCE HALL

FREE TICKETS
FOR RIDES
Will Be Available At
The Log Cabin—Euclid Beach Park

FREE DANCING
IN THE
MAIN DANCE HALL
8:30 - 11:00
★
MUSIC BY
HARRY HERSHEY
and His Orchestra

90